Columbia University

Contributions to Education

Teachers College Series

No. 166

AMS PRESS
NEW YORK

THE RELATION BETWEEN GRADE SCHOOL RECORD AND HIGH SCHOOL ACHIEVEMENT

A STUDY OF THE DIAGNOSTIC VALUE OF INDIVIDUAL RECORD CARDS

BY

CLAY CAMPBELL ROSS, Ph.D.
ASSISTANT PROFESSOR OF PSYCHOLOGY, IOWA STATE COLLEGE

TEACHERS COLLEGE, COLUMBIA UNIVERSITY
CONTRIBUTIONS TO EDUCATION, NO. 166

Published by

𝕿eachers College, Columbia University
New York City
1925

Library of Congress Cataloging in Publication Data

Ross, Clay Campbell, 1892-1947.
　The relation between grade school record and high
school achievement.

　Reprint of the 1925 ed., issued in series: Teachers
College, Columbia University. Contributions to educa-
tion, no. 166.
　Originally presented as the author's thesis, Columbia.

　Includes bibliographical references.
　1. Prediction of scholastic success. 2. Personnel
records in education. I. Title. II. Series: Columbia
University. Teachers College. Contributions to education, no. 166.
LB1131.R593　1972　　　371.2'64　　　　70-177211
ISBN 0-404-55166-1

Reprinted by Special Arrangement with Teachers
College Press, New York, New York

From the edition of 1925, New York
First AMS edition published in 1972
Manufactured in the United States

AMS PRESS, INC.
NEW YORK, N. Y.　10003

ACKNOWLEDGMENT

While it is not possible to mention specifically all who have coöperated in the making of this study, the writer wishes to acknowledge his special indebtedness to Professors N. L. Engelhardt, Arthur I. Gates, and Thomas H. Briggs, under whose helpful counsel and direction the study was made; to Superintendent Albert Leonard, the principals, and teachers of the elementary and high schools of New Rochelle, N. Y., and to Superintendent J. W. Studebaker, the principals, and teachers of the elementary and high schools of Des Moines, Iowa, who generously placed their school records at his disposal, and whose unfailing courtesy and patience alone made possible the collection of the data; and to Dr. Herbert A. Toops, who first suggested the problem, and whose statistical genius and contagious enthusiasm have been a guide and inspiration throughout.

C. C. R.

CONTENTS

TABLES

FIGURES

THE RELATION BETWEEN GRADE SCHOOL RECORD AND HIGH SCHOOL ACHIEVEMENT

CHAPTER I

THE PROBLEM

The first two decades of the twentieth century have witnessed a rapid development of the scientific study of education. During this period students of education have either devised their own tools and techniques of experimentation and research, or have taken over some of the tools and techniques already applied to other fields. Among the most important of these developments have been the construction of more exact instruments for measuring educational achievements and the application of statistical methods to the study of educational data.

While educational psychologists have always taken a very prominent part in this movement, its applications have been largely directed to the problems of educational administration. Of these administrative problems two have been brought into bold relief by the tremendous increase in our school enrollments, which more than ever include pupils of widely varying interests and capacities, particularly in the high school, together with the greatly multiplied curricular offerings accompanying this increase. One of these problems is that of adequate guidance, both educational and vocational, and the other is that of sectioning these pupils into homeogeneous groups for instructional purposes. The solution of both of these problems depends upon the discovery of satisfactory bases for predicting academic success.

Several studies have been made in an effort to find answers to these fundamental questions: "Can academic success be predicted? If so, how? To what extent can previous scholastic success be used as a basis for prediction?" One of the earliest and best known of these studies was made fifteen years ago by Dearborn,[1] who found that in 75 per cent of the cases the standing of pupils in the

[1] Dearborn, W. F., *Relative Standing of Pupils in the High School and in the University*, Bulletin No. 312, University of Wisconsin, 1909.

university can be predicted from the standing in the high school. Other studies of the relation between high school and college standing have since been made by Smith,[1] Lincoln,[2] and others. In a similar manner the relation between the standing of pupils in the elementary and high schools have been studied by Carter,[3] Miles,[4] and others. All of these investigators have employed the method of simple correlations and have been concerned primarily with the relation between the *average standing* in the two types of schools being compared.

Then in 1914 came Kelley's *Educational Guidance*,[5] which brought to the attention of students of the problem the wonderful possibilities of multiple correlations. This technique made it possible for the first time to combine the separate details of a pupil's record according to the relative importance of each as a factor in prognosis. This method of combining the factors yielded a higher measure of prediction than could be obtained by a correlation of the simple arithmetical average of all factors without regard to their relative importance. About this time, however, studies by Kelly,[6] Starch[7] and Elliot, and others tended to bring teachers' marks somewhat into disrepute. These studies, together with the rapid development of standard tests, have served to divert the current of investigation away from the ordinary records of the pupils and into the field of special measurements. Among typical representatives of these later studies relating to educational prognosis may be mentioned those of Fretwell,[8] Rogers,[9] and Allen.[10] As a result of this change in emphasis the possibilities of multiple correlation tech-

[1] Smith, F. O., *A Rational Basis for Determining Fitness for College Entrance*, University of Iowa Studies, Vol. I, 1910.

[2] Lincoln, E. A., "The Relative Standing of Pupils in High School, in Early College, and in College Entrance Examinations," *School and Society*, Vol. V, p. 417, 1917.

[3] Carter, R. E., "Correlation of Elementary Schools and High School," *Elementary School Teacher*, Vol. XII, pp. 109–118.

[4] Miles, W. R., *Comparison of Elementary and High School Grades*, University of Iowa Studies in Education, Vol. I, 1910.

[5] Kelley, T. L., *Educational Guidance*, Teachers College, Columbia University, Contributions to Education, No. 71, New York, 1914.

[6] Kelly, F. J., *Teachers Marks*, Teachers College, Columbia University, Contributions to Education, No. 66, New York, 1914.

[7] Starch, Daniel, *Educational Psychology*, pp. 433–435, The MacMillan Company, New York, 1919.

[8] Fretwell, E. K., *A Study in Educational Prognosis*, Teachers College, Columbia University, Contributions to Education, No. 99, New York, 1919.

[9] Rogers, Agnes L., *Experimental Tests of Mathematical Ability and Their Prognostic Value*, Teachers College, Columbia University, Contributions to Education, No. 89, New York, 1918.

[10] Allen, W. S., *A Study in Latin Prognosis*, Teachers College, Columbia University, Contributions to Education, No. 135, New York, 1923.

nique when applied to the relation between the ordinary facts of the grade school record and later school achievement have not been tested out.

The present study returns to the problem of determining the relation between a pupil's record in the grade school and his later achievement in the high school. A more detailed analysis of the problem has been attempted than has heretofore appeared. Answers to two major questions have been sought: First, what is the relation between a pupil's grade school record and his success in the high school? Second, what is the relation between a pupil's grade school record and his length of stay in the high school? The first of these problems has been resolved into several specific questions: What is the relation between the separate elements of the grade school record and the pupil's average standing in the high school? What is the relation of these separate elements of the grade school record and the pupil's standing in the individual subjects, English, Latin, and mathematics? What combination of these factors will best enable us to predict the standing in high school of pupils in the first year of the high school, and in the subjects, English, Latin, and mathematics? What combination will best enable us to predict the standing in high school of pupils who remain longer than one year?

The second problem has also been resolved into specific questions: In what respects, and to what extent, does the grade school record of pupils who graduate from high school differ from those of pupils who complete the eighth grade but do not enter high school; from those of pupils who drop out of high school during or at the end of the first year; and from those of pupils who remain in high school longer than one year but who never graduate? What combination of these factors will give us the best measure of prediction of a pupil's probable stay in high school?

The nature and source of the data used are described in Chapter II; the relation between the pupil's grade school record and high school success will be considered in Chapter III; and the relation between the pupil's grade school record and persistence in high school will be considered in Chapter IV. Chapter V gives a general summary of the entire study.

CHAPTER II

THE NATURE AND SOURCE OF THE DATA

THE INDIVIDUAL RECORD CARD IN THE GRADE SCHOOL

One of the significant tendencies in recent educational practice has been the increased attention given to records and reports. Along with the construction of standard tests and the application of statistical methods to educational data has come pronounced improvement in school records and reports of all kinds. One of the most important of these records has been the development of an individual pupil record card which contains the entire educational history of the pupil from the day he enters school till he has completed the eighth grade. That these records are of great value while the pupil is still in the elementary school is clear enough, but as these cards rarely ever accompany the pupil when he reports to high school, and are, indeed, seldom used for any purpose whatsoever, once the pupil is out of the grade school, their later usefulness is open to question. Notwithstanding this, these records are generally stored away in some safe place where they are still regarded with a certain mysterious awe, for school officials *feel* they still have value, even if they are by no means sure just what this value is.

For years, however, psychologists have been telling us we are bundles of habits—that the body of information, skills, interests, attitudes, and the like, that we acquire in the form of experience determines in large measure the kind of people we are today and will be tomorrow. But no one believes that all parts of this experience are of equal value in shaping our futures, and the problem is to find out what factors are most significant for this purpose. That the entries on these individual record cards are records of the experience of these pupils during the formative years while they are in the grade school, and so may be of great value in predicting their future, as undoubtedly the experience itself is of tremendous influence in determining this future, seems reasonable enough. Such a relationship is especially probable when we confine ourselves to predicting their future record *in school*.

A glance at the information contained on one of these cards will reveal its pertinency. Here we find the following facts: Pupil's name, address, date of birth, date of entering school, age at entering school, date of leaving or completing school, age at leaving or completing school, number of semesters accelerated or retarded, teachers' marks by grades in the various school subjects, records of attendance, deportment, effort, and transfers. The different types of these cards vary somewhat among themselves, but practically any standard form will contain the above items, and some have considerably more.

It is obvious that the bulk of the record is that of teachers' marks, and the objection may be immediately raised that these are so hopelessly unreliable as to preclude any possibility of use. It is undoubtedly true, as has been pointed out by Kelly, Starch, and others, that there are wide differences in the individual ratings of a single paper, and the relative values assigned to individual questions, and the like. But one fact is often overlooked, namely, that it is one thing to assign an absolute value to a question or paper, and quite another thing to estimate its relative value. Teachers may not be able to agree as to whether a pupil is due 78 or 87 on a single examination paper, and yet have little difficulty in agreeing that the pupil is better or poorer than other members of the class. When a teacher has been with a group of children for a year, she is likely to be able to differentiate between the poor, average, good, and excellent ones, even though she might not agree with another teacher as to the exact numerical value of the varying degrees of achievement. Moreover, by the time a pupil has completed the grade school, the record card normally contains the ratings of eight or more teachers, and so amounts to a group judgment as to his scholastic achievement. Even one so uncompromisingly skeptical of the value of teachers' marks as F. J. Kelly concedes this. On this point Kelly[1] says: "We should expect the average of the estimates of a dozen or more teachers to come pretty close to the correct ranking of young people. We should expect the average estimate of a dozen teachers in the higher school to come pretty close to the same ranking."

Those who have been most prompt in recognizing the value of standard tests and most prominent in developing them, recognize that teachers' marks are not without merit. Tests are standardized

[1] Kelly, F. J., *op. cit.*, p. 20.

in relation to teachers' estimates of pupils' achievements. Obviously, if standard tests correlate with teachers' marks, then teachers' marks correlate with standard tests. No less a statistical authority than T. L. Kelley says of teachers' marks:[1] "In the attempt to meet these demands (those of guidance), and to meet them on the spot and without a moment's delay, one of the richest sources of information is likely to be only very partially utilized. Reference is made to that product accumulated by every pupil—school grades. Whatever capacity it is that a grade, say, in mathematics, stands for, it is measured with a high degree of accuracy when the records of several years and of several teachers are combined. A pupil's record is the most complete, detailed and accurate of all records of the ordinary pupil from his entrance in school to his entrance into work."

Another value of these marks, accumulated as they are from grade to grade by different teachers, is that they give a picture of the pupil under varying conditions and stages of development. Biologists recognize that competent observers of the life history of an organism often get a more valuable and complete understanding of the organism than can be had from a single laboratory experiment, however careful and painstaking the latter may be. In this connection William James says:[2] "No elementary measurement, capable of being performed in a laboratory, can throw any light on the actual efficiency of the subject; for the vital thing about him, his emotional and moral doggedness, can be measured by no single experiment, and becomes known only by the total results in the long run." In the record card we have, so to speak, many stages of unfoldment of the individual, recorded under normal conditions from time to time; while the special battery of tests partakes more of the nature of the laboratory experiment, giving us a cross-section of the individual's experience at some particular point.

No disparagement of standard tests is intended; quite the contrary. The only desire of the writer is to point out that cumulative records have certain peculiar merits of their own that must not be overlooked. But here, as in biology, neither the record of the life history of the organism nor the detailed laboratory experiment, is complete when used alone, and complete knowledge will only come from uniting the two. No attempt is made to gloss over the defects

---

[1] Kelley, T. L., *op. cit.*, p. 84.
[2] James, Wm. *Talks to Teachers*, p. 135, New York, 1899.

of subjective estimates by teachers. That they are subject to inaccuracies no one familiar with the situation will deny. But correlations based upon teachers' marks, because of these inaccuracies, will tend to be smaller than is warranted by the actual degree of relationship, were more reliable measures available. Thorndike[1] states the effect of attenuation as follows: "The influence of chance inaccuracy in the measures to be related is always to produce zero correlation." If these ratings on the pupil's individual record card were truly objective measures of the pupil's achievement while in the grade school, as would result from the use of standard tests in making up the ratings as they accumulate year by year, we might reasonably expect higher correlations with high school achievement than ordinary marks yield. Unfortunately, standard tests have not been in wide use long enough to make possible a study of this kind based wholly upon such ratings. That remains for the future. For the present we must rely for our data upon teachers' marks which we shall find are by no means unfruitful.

WHY NEW ROCHELLE WAS SELECTED FOR THIS STUDY

The scope of the investigation having been decided upon, the first problem was to find a place where these records had been kept over a period of years. In order to trace the relationships desired, it was necessary to go back far enough to permit even the slow pupils either to finish high school or drop out of school altogether. The plan was to take a series of classes completing the eighth grade and trace their subsequent educational history with the hope of discovering relationships between this and the grade school record. With this in view letters were sent to some thirty cities in the vicinity of New York City, inquiring whether the desired records were available. In addition to this the writer visited ten places in person. All of these cities expressed willingness to coöperate but only three cities appeared to have the records needed for the study. Owing to the limitations of time, it was necessary to make a choice between taking a group from each of the three cities for a single year, or successive groups from a single city. The latter course appeared the more feasible, the plan decided upon being to study the complete records of all pupils who had completed the eighth grade during the years 1916, 1917, 1918, and 1919, and who had been in

[1] Thorndike, E. L., *An Introduction to the Theory of Mental and Social Measurements*, p. 178. Revised Edition, New York, 1913.

the local school system at least from the beginning of the third grade. After the advantages and disadvantages of each of the three cities were weighed, New Rochelle, New York, was selected as the most suitable place for the study. One of the conditions at New Rochelle that made it especially favorable for the study was that the city had enjoyed a continuous and progressive educational policy and administration for many years. Principals of the individual schools, as well as the city superintendent, have occupied their present positions during practically the entire period covered by the present study, so that we have a more consistent system of records and reports than would be possible under the vicissitudes of changing administrations.

New Rochelle is a city of about 40,000 population, situated in Westchester County, New York, eighteen miles from New York City. It is a well-to-do residential city, with very few industries, but it is probably typical of the suburban communities around New York City. In most of Burdge's[1] tables showing the comparative standing of the cities of New York State as regards sixteen-, seventeen-, and eighteen-year-old employed boys, New Rochelle, along with White Plains, Mt. Vernon, and other cities in the vicinity, ranks not far from the median position, though usually somewhat on the more favorable side.

SECURING THE INFORMATION

The first step was to secure a transcript of the grade school records of all pupils who had completed the eighth grade, and who had been in the city schools since the beginning of third grade and the high school records of those who went to high school. For this purpose the card reproduced in Figure 1 was devised, which presents in a compact and accessible form all the necessary facts of both records.

At the top of the card appear the pupil's name and the name and address of his parent or guardian, these for the purpose of identification. Then comes the date of birth from which it is easy to calculate the age of pupil at entering school and his age at the completion of the eighth grade. It was discovered, however, that the age at entering school would be of little value for our purpose, owing to the fact that so many pupils entered the system later

[1] Burdge, H. G., *Our Boys. A Study of 245,000 Sixteen, Seventeen, and Eighteen Year Old Employed Boys of the State of New York*, Albany, 1921.

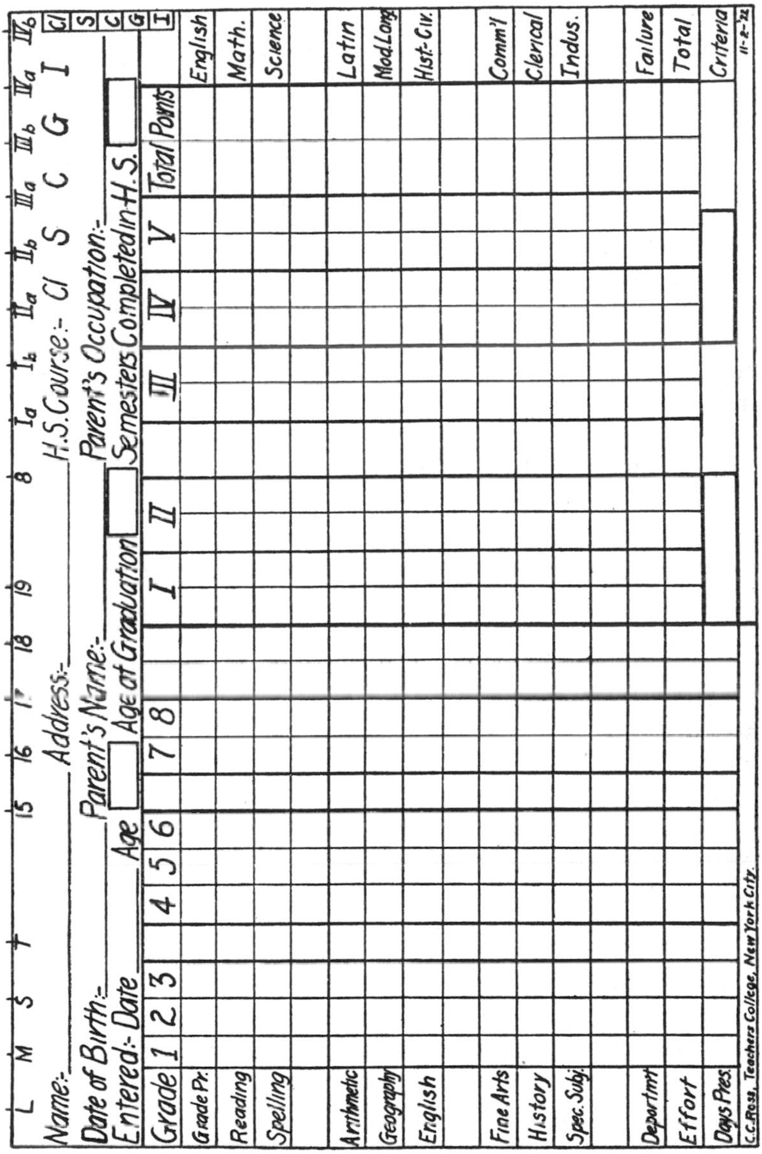

FIGURE 1. CUMULATIVE RECORD CARD USED IN THE STUDY

than the first grade. The heavy vertical line down the center of the card separates the grade school record on the left from the high school record on the right. The former is entered by grades, the average being taken of the semester marks for each subject, while the latter is recorded by semesters exactly as it appeared on the original record. Three items require explanation: "Grade-Progress" means the number of semesters accelerated or retarded, a semester accelerated being indicated at the proper place by a 1 and a semester retarded by a − 1; "Fine Arts" is the average of music and drawing combined; and "Special Subjects" is the average of physical education and manual training combined.

A few of the mechanical features of the card may be of interest. It will be observed that these entries are grouped by threes, both horizontally and vertically, with a space between groups. This serves the purpose both of aiding the eye in recording the data and later in tabulating it. It also provides a convenient space for entering in red ink the average of grade-groups. At the top of the card appear the letters L, M, S, T, which are the initial letters of the four large elementary schools, and the numbers 15, 16, 17, 18, 19, which are contractions for 1915, 1916, 1917, 1918, 1919, and which indicate the year when the pupil completed the eighth grade. In a similar manner the letters 8*a*, I*a*, I*b*, II*a*, II*b*, etc., indicate the last grade completed in school. In filling out these items on the card the proper designations were made by simply putting a circle around the proper school, year, and grade. Later, by means of a card-punch the marginal edge of each of these circles was clipped away so that one could see by a glance at a pack of cards their proper designations. This simple device aided materially in preventing the mixing of cards by providing a ready and sure means of identification. The letters Cl, G, S, C, and I, at the right edge of the card near the top, represented the four curricula offered by the New Rochelle High School, namely, classical, general, scientific, commercial, and industrial. These were indicated in the same manner as the school, year and grade. In order to make it easy to keep the records of boys and girls separate, a buff card was used for boys and a white card for girls.

On the original cards the grade school entries were in letters, A, B, C, D, and F, which had the numerical values, respectively, 90–100, 80–90, 75–80, 65–75, and "under 65." In this study an F is arbitrarily placed at 60, and the other grades are regarded as having the value of the mid-point of the interval. All averages ranged from 65, which was barely passing, to 99. In order to facilitate the statistical handling of the data, in recording the grades on the new cards, transmuted values were used instead of the actual gross scores, as appears in the table below.

Gross Score	Transmuted Score
97–99	11
94–96	10
91–93	9
88–90	8
85–87	7
82–84	6
79–81	5
76–78	4
73–75	3
70–72	2
67–69	1
64–66	0

A similar table of transmuted values was used for recording number of days in attendance during the school year.

Days Attendance	Transmuted Score
195–204	9
185–194	8
175–184	7
165–174	6
155–164	5
145–154	4
135–144	3
125–134	2
115–124	1
105–114	0

These tables merely code the original records by transmuting them into class intervals, or "steps," which may again be converted to the original scores when so desired.[1] The means and S.D.'s used in all correlations are in terms of these transmuted, or class-interval scores, while the means and medians used in comparing the means and overlappings of the different groups are in terms of the actual gross scores. Grade-progress and age at completing the eighth

[1] For the details of this method, see Toops, H. A., "Computing Intercorrelations on the Adding Machine," *Journal of Applied Psychology*, Vol. VI, pp. 172–176, 1922.

grade, calculated in half-years to nearest birthday, were originally entered in actual gross scores, but were later converted into transmuted scores according to the tables given below.

AGE AT COMPLETING EIGHTH GRADE		GRADE-PROGRESS	
Age in Years	Transmuted Score	Total Semesters	Transmuted Score
17	10	4	7
16½	9	3	6
16	8	2	5
15½	7	1	4
15	6	0	3
14½	5	−1	2
14	4	−2	1
13½	3	−3	0
13	2		
12½	1		
12	0		

By using methods which will be described more fully in Chapter III, the writer was able to follow up the complete school history of more than 99 per cent of the pupils who completed the eighth grade in New Rochelle during the years 1916, 1917, 1918, and 1919. The summary below gives the total number of cases involved, 749 in all, arranged in groups according to length of stay in high school, for the four years.

Group	1916	1917	1918	1919	Total
Number Graduating from High School....	57	71	78	110	316
Number not Entering High School.......	22	42	50	30	144
Number Remaining in High School One Year or Less.........................	30	51	27	23	131
Number Remaining in High School over One Year, but not Graduating..........	32	36	59	31	158
Total Number Completing Eighth Grade...	141	200	214	194	749

CHAPTER III

THE RELATION BETWEEN GRADE SCHOOL RECORD AND HIGH SCHOOL SUCCESS

The questions this chapter proposes to consider are as follows:

1. What is the relation between each of the factors of a pupil's grade school record and his average standing in the first year of high school?

2. What is the relation between each of the factors of a pupil's grade school record and his success in the individual subjects, English, mathematics, and Latin, in the first year of high school?

3. What combination of these factors will give us the best measure of prediction of a pupil's average standing in the first year of high school?

4. What combination of these factors will give us the best measure of prediction of a pupil's standing in English, mathematics, and Latin in the first year of high school?

5. What combination of these factors will yield the best measure of prediction of average success in high school of those pupils who remain two or more years?

6. What combination of these factors will yield the best measure of prediction of the average success in English for those pupils who remain two or more years in high school?

A GENERAL STATEMENT REGARDING METHOD

The technique employed in determining the relation between the grade school record and high school success is that of simple and multiple correlations. In the former case the Toops[1] method of solving the Pearson formula has been followed, and in the latter case the Toops[2] multiple ratio correlation technique has been followed. The discussion throughout will be as non-technical as

[1] Toops, H. A., "Eliminating the Pitfalls in Solving Correlation: A Printed Correlation Form," *Journal of Experimental Psychology*, pp. 434–446, Vol. IV, 1912.

[2] Toops, H. A., *Tests for Vocational Guidance of Children Thirteen to Sixteen*, Teachers College, Columbia University, Contributions to Education, No. 136, pp. 137–153, New York, 1923. For briefer discussions see Allen, W. S., *op. cit.*, pp. 18–25, and Garfiel, Evelyn, "The Measurements of Motor Ability," Archives of Psychology, No. 62, pp. 18–21, New York, 1923.

possible and no statistical knowledge on the part of the reader beyond that of an understanding of simple correlations has been presupposed. Those interested in the more technical phases of the statistical treatment employed are referred to the original sources where both the simple and multiple correlation procedures are discussed at length.

In one respect, however, the plan followed here has been unique. Instead of throwing all the data together and considering the four years as a whole, the writer has chosen the year 1917 as the basal year, and all relationships have first been determined for that year; afterwards these prediction formulas have been applied to the year preceding, and to the two years following 1917. In this way it has been found possible to secure a measure of the stability and general trustworthiness of the regression equations when applied to this kind of data that would not have been possible otherwise.

RELATION BETWEEN GRADE SCHOOL RECORD AND SUCCESS IN THE FIRST YEAR OF HIGH SCHOOL

What is the relation between the separate items of a pupil's grade school record and his subsequent record in the first year of high school? To answer in detail this question alone would require several hundred correlations. What we are especially interested in, however, is to discover what factors are most directly related with high school success in the first year. This, happily, is a very much simpler problem.

The grades in high school were recorded by semesters in letters as follows: A+, A, B+, B, C+, C, D+, D, F, with percentage values, respectively, 95–100, 90–94, 85–89, 80–84, 75–79, 70–74, 65–69, 60–64, under 60. In this study these letters are assigned the arbitrary values, respectively, 8, 7, 6, 5, 4, 3, 2, 1, 0, and the two semester ratings are combined to give the standing in each subject for the year. The average of these subject ratings gives the average standing of the pupil in high school for the year.

Table I shows for the year 1917 the correlation of the average school mark made throughout the grade school in each of the subjects studied with the average standing in the first year of high school, and with the record in the individual subjects English and mathematics. There are 134 cases in this group; Latin with only 57 cases is not included here. Since the record in the first grade

TABLE I

CORRELATIONS BETWEEN AVERAGE SCHOOL MARK IN THE VARIOUS
GRADE SCHOOL SUBJECTS AND THREE CRITERIA OF SUCCESS
IN THE FIRST YEAR OF HIGH SCHOOL

$N = 134$

Subject in the Grade School*	Criterion Correlations		
	Average	English	Mathematics
Reading.....................	.35	.46	.18
Spelling.....................	.36	.45	.18
Arithmetic..................	.52	.44	.38
Geography..................	.50	.50	.28
English.....................	.59	.50	.34
Fine Arts...................	.35	.48	.08
History.....................	.40	.40	.24
Special Subjects............	.26	.43	.03
Deportment.................	.35	.45	.15
Effort......................	.37	.50	.17
Days Present...............	.00	.05	.02
Average All Subjects........	.60	.66	.30

* Every subject except geography and history is taught in all grades.

was lacking on so many cards it was omitted from consideration in order to make the averages comparable.

It is reasonable to assume that there is some variation between the correlations of the different grades in any one subject with high school success. To discover which of the grades are most highly correlated with success in the first year of high school, the two subjects, English and arithmetic, whose average for the entire grade school period correlates highest with the three criteria of high school success, were correlated with these same criteria both by grades and by grade-groups. These results are given in Table II and in Table III.

It will be seen that the correlations of the grade-groups 2–3, 4–6, 7–8 are in every case higher than the average of the correlations of the grades composing the group when computed separately. In most cases they are higher than the correlation of any particular grade of the grade-group; and in no case is the correlation of a grade more than .03 higher than that of the grade-group of which

TABLE II

CORRELATIONS BETWEEN ENGLISH AND THREE CRITERIA OF
SUCCESS IN THE FIRST YEAR OF HIGH SCHOOL, BOTH BY
GRADES AND BY GRADE-GROUPS

$N = 134$

English by Grades	Criterion Correlations		
	Average	English	Mathematics
Grade 2...................	.31	.38	.09
Grade 3...................	.34	.39	.13
Grade-Group 2–3...........	.50	.43	.12
Grade 4...................	.48	.53	.28
Grade 5...................	.39	.37	.19
Grade 6...................	.47	.42	.31
Grade-Group 4–6...........	.56	.54	.34
Grade 7...................	.46	.46	.26
Grade 8...................	.48	.51	.34
Grade-Group 7–8...........	.54	.53	.35
Grade-Group 2–8...........	.59	.50	.34

TABLE III

CORRELATIONS BETWEEN ARITHMETIC AND THREE CRITERIA
OF SUCCESS IN THE FIRST YEAR OF HIGH SCHOOL, BOTH BY
GRADES AND BY GRADE-GROUPS

$N = 134$

Arithmetic by Grades	Criterion Correlations		
	Average	English	Mathematics
Grade 2...................	.22	.34	.10
Grade 3...................	.25	.20	.15
Grade-Group 2–3...........	.27	.32	.13
Grade 4...................	.35	.26	.25
Grade 5...................	.28	.17	.19
Grade 6...................	.45	.28	.35
Grade-Group 4–6...........	.44	.30	.32
Grade 7...................	.41	.37	.32
Grade 8...................	.52	.49	.39
Grade-Group 7–8...........	.53	.48	.42
Grade-Group 2–8...........	.52	.44	.38

it is a part. Therefore, even if it were not manifestly impossible to carry the correlations of each subject for each grade throughout the study, apparently little or nothing would be gained from so doing. In fact, the correlations with marks by grade-groups, combining as they do the judgments of two or more teachers in each case, have a distinct advantage the other method would not possess. From this point on in the study, therefore, the factors considered will be those of grade-groups, except in the case of grade-progress which is the total number of semesters gained or lost during grades 2 to 8, combined algebraically, and in the case of age at completing the eighth grade. The correlation of these factors to be considered hereafter, with average success in the first year of high school, and with success in English, mathematics, and Latin during the first year of high school are given in Table IV.

The negative correlations in Table IV are likely to attract attention first of all, and are therefore perhaps worthy of special comment. It has been pointed out often that a pupil's chronological age is correlated negatively with his standing in school. But this is not difficult to explain, as many of the older pupils at the time of completing the eighth grade are old by reason of being dull and thereby having to repeat the work in some of the grades; or they may have developed habits of idleness and indifference, which held them back.

This, however, is not the case with school attendance. It may be surprising to find that the number of days present correlates negatively with school success in every case except two, and here the positive correlations are very slight. Absence for brief periods seems to favor success in high school, being apparently, the pardonable offense of the capable pupils, whose parents keep them at home a day or so now and then for entirely legitimate reasons — illness, for example — and who are able to make up the work covered by the class while they were away. Absence in and of itself is probably not a virtue, but for brief periods it seems to be associated with abilities that do make for high school success. It seems probable, however, that pupils who are absent a great deal are never able to complete the grade school at all. Some evidence in support of this is afforded by the fact that relatively few pupils who have been absent during each school grade on the average of as much as a month have completed the eighth grade and appear in this study. However, it would seem that we must qualify the opinion that

TABLE IV

CORRELATION OF EACH FACTOR WITH SUCCESS IN THE FIRST YEAR
OF HIGH SCHOOL, TOGETHER WITH THE MEANS AND S.D.'S
OF EACH DISTRIBUTION

$N = 134$, except in case of Latin, where $N = 57$
1917 Group

Factor	Criterion Correlations				Mean*	S.D.*
	Average	English	Math.	Latin		
Age at End Gr. 8.............	—.36	—.38	—.26	—.25	3.5	2.0
Grade-Progress...............	.39	.36	.22	.32	3.8	1.2
Reading, Gr. 2–3.............	.29	.41	.15	.26	8.3	1.7
Reading, Gr. 4–6.............	.31	.41	.15	.12	8.2	1.7
Reading, Gr. 7–8.............	.38	.44	.18	.28	8.3	1.5
Spelling, Gr. 2–3.............	.30	.45	.12	.42	8.5	1.8
Spelling, Gr. 4–6.............	.33	.39	.15	.28	8.6	1.6
Spelling, Gr. 7–8.............	.28	.30	.18	.33	8.4	2.0
Arithmetic, Gr. 2–3...........	.27	.32	.13	.36	7.5	2.0
Arithmetic, Gr. 4–6...........	.44	.30	.32	.37	6.6	2.0
Arithmetic, Gr. 7–8..........	.53	.48	.42	.52	6.6	2.3
Geography, Gr. 4–6..........	.52	.50	.32	.41	7.3	1.7
History, Gr. 5–6.............	.38	.36	.04	.52	7.1	1.7
History, Gr. 7–8.............	.37	.39	.23	.49	7.3	1.9
English, Gr. 2–3.............	.50	.43	.18	.23	7.7	1.6
English, Gr. 4–6.............	.56	.54	.12	.48	7.2	1.6
English, Gr. 7–8.............	.54	.53	.34	.54	6.9	1.8
Fine Arts, Gr. 2–3...........	.31	.39	.35	.18	7.4	1.6
Fine Arts, Gr. 4–6...........	.39	.45	.11	.17	7.2	1.4
Fine Arts, Gr. 7–8...........	.27	.36	.13	—.01	7.7	1.5
Spec. Subjects, Gr. 2–3.·.....	.14	.21	.25	.11	8.5	1.4
Spec. Subjects, Gr. 4–6.......	.30	.47	.05	.06	8.2	1.2
Spec. Subjects, Gr. 7–8.......	.22	.38	.08	.09	8.2	1.2
Deportment, Gr. 2–3.........	.26	.30	.06	.07	8.7	1.6
Deportment, Gr. 4–6.........	.33	.45	.11	.21	8.6	1.5
Deportment, Gr. 7–8.........	.33	.35	.14	.24	8.6	1.7
Effort, Gr. 2–3..............	.21	.30	.00	.14	9.0	1.4
Effort, Gr. 4–6..............	.37	.42	.13	.22	8.9	1.2
Effort, Gr. 7–8..............	.46	.37	.22	.12	8.9	1.4
Days Present, Gr. 2–3........	—.03	—.06	.10	—.06	7.0	1.3
Days Present, Gr. 4–6........	—.11	—.14	—.10	—.14	7.9	1.0
Days Present, Gr. 7–8........	—.01	—.05	.01	—.04	8.5	1.0

* All means and S.D.'s are in terms of transmuted scores. For example, the true values for age are 13.8 years and 1.0 year, respectively, and the true values for grade-progress are .8 semesters and 1.2 semesters, respectively.

certain students who have studied the problem of attendance have expressed. For example, Reavis[1] says: "Attendance is the most important determining factor of quality of work." But Reavis' statement becomes much less impressive when we discover that the correlation between attendance and quality of work in rural schools for pupils over seven years of age is between .20 and .25,[2] while the median correlation between other factors of the grade school record and success in the first year of high school, as shown in Table IV, are higher than that except in one case.

From the correlations in Table IV it is clear that the factors of the grade school record vary considerably in their relation to the different subjects in the high school, as well as among themselves in relation to any one subject. The correlations of the several factors of the grade school record with the average standing in the first year of the high school range from —.36 to +.56, with English the range is from —.38 to +.54, with mathematics the range is from —.26 to +.42, and with Latin the range is from .25 to +.54. The median correlations are, respectively, .33, .39, .15, and .24.

What we are especially interested in, however, is not the magnitude of the correlations when taken individually, but rather the degree of prediction that is possible when we combine the factors into groups, or teams. We shall now attempt to discover the best combination of these factors which will afford the best measure of prediction of success in the first year of high school.

PREDICTING FIRST YEAR HIGH SCHOOL SUCCESS FROM GRADE SCHOOL RECORD

We have already seen that a simple average of all marks received during the entire grade-school period gives a correlation of .60 with average standing in the first year of high school. This grade school average, however, combines factors which separately correlate much below .60, as is seen in Table IV, and so have the effect of reducing the correlation of the average of which they are a part. Furthermore, all factors entering into the average influence it equally, regardless of their actual correlation with it, the magnitude of which has been seen to vary considerably. Our problem is to

[1] Reavis, G. H., *Factors Controlling Attendance in Rural Schools*, Teachers College, Columbia University, Contributions to Education, No. 108, p. 14, New York, 1920.
[2] *Ibid.*, p. 13.

discover, therefore, which group of these factors, when combined at their optimum weight or value, will give the highest measure of prediction. The Toops multiple ratio correlation procedure performs just this service, and gives us an approximate multiple correlation which will not vary from the true R by more than .01. Beginning with the factor which correlates highest individually with the criterion, this procedure locates successively, in descending order, the factors, which, when combined with other factors already so selected, will give the highest correlation. It also determines the proper weight of each factor added to the composite, and indicates the magnitude of the correlation at each stage of the operation. Moreover, this procedure necessitates finding only the correlation of the factors found significant with all the other factors, and not all of the intercorrelations, as does the longer method of obtaining the true R.

Table V gives the correlation of each of the ten most significant factors with every other factor. Miles[1] reported that pupils making good marks in one subject tended to make good marks in all subjects, but he does not venture an opinion as to whether this was due to any inherent tendency for all good things to be correlated or is merely the effect of some "halo" that is shed over a pupil's entire record by excellence in some one particular subject. Whatever the cause may have been in Miles' study, that same condition is not found here. In fact, some may judge from the size of these intercorrelations among the factors of a pupil's record in the grade school that there is an alarming amount of disagreement among teachers concerning the achievements of a single pupil! Some light may be thrown upon this question, however, by comparing the magnitude of these correlations with the correlations Fretwell[2] obtained between various standard tests and the same or similar tests repeated one year later in the junior high school. In that study the correlations ranged from .22 to .56, with a central tendency of .38. Henmon[3] also reports that the intercorrelations of seven history tests range from —.08 to .76 and those of seven comprehension tests in reading range from .02 to .77, with an average of .40 for each group, and few would disagree with his conclusion that such results are "at best discouraging."

[1] Miles, *op. cit.*, p. 10.
[2] Fretwell, *op. cit.*, p. 25.
[3] Henmon, V. A. C., "Some Limitations of Educational Tests," *Journal of Educational Research*, pp. 185–198, March, 1923.

TABLE V

CORRELATION OF EACH OF THE TEN FACTORS MOST SIGNIFICANT
IN PREDICTING HIGH SCHOOL SUCCESS WITH EVERY
OTHER FACTOR

Factor	Age at End Gr. 8	Grade-Progress	Arithmetic Gr. 7-8	English Gr. 4-6	English Gr. 7-8	Spec. Sub. Gr. 4-6	Spec. Sub. Gr. 7-8	Effort Gr. 7-8	Days Pres. Gr. 2-3	Days Pres. Gr. 4-6
Age at End Gr. 8	....	—.44	—.30	—.33	—.30	—.12	—.03	—.09	.03	—.05
Grade-Progress	—.44	....	.23	.48	.23	.27	.14	.18	.03	.10
Arithmetic, Gr. 7-8	—.30	.23	....	.46	.62	.17	.17	.34	—.03	.02
English, Gr. 4-6	—.33	.48	.46	....	.56	.35	.25	.34	—.06	.00
English, Gr. 7-8	—.30	.23	.62	.56	....	.18	.18	.45	—.05	—.17
Spec. Subjects, Gr. 4-6	—.12	.27	.17	.35	.18	....	.48	.38	.09	.13
Spec. Subjects, Gr. 7-8	—.03	.14	.17	.25	.18	.48	....	.38	—.02	.13
Effort, Gr. 7-8	—.09	.18	.34	.34	.45	.38	.38	....	.15	.04
Days Present, Gr. 2-3	.03	.03	—.03	—.06	—.05	.09	—.02	.15	....	.25
Days Present, Gr. 4-6	—.05	.10	.02	.00	—.17	.13	.13	.04	.25	....
Geography, Gr. 4-6	—.39	.58	.52	.71	.51	.31	.15	.26	.03	.10
Reading, Gr. 2-3	—.43	.39	.28	.53	.38	.15	.10	.05	—.13	—.06
Reading, Gr. 4-6	—.41	.29	.26	.62	.42	.22	.10	.09	—.16	—.16
Reading, Gr. 7-8	—.33	.29	.34	.55	.54	.15	.31	.20	—.13	—.16
Spelling, Gr. 2-3	—.37	.41	.27	.52	.38	.35	.27	.23	—.04	.04
Spelling, Gr. 4-6	—.33	.31	.27	.60	.37	.33	.22	.25	—.04	.10
Spelling, Gr. 7-8	—.24	.23	.36	.51	.43	.12	.12	.18	—.16	.02
Arithmetic, Gr. 2-3	—.17	.35	.41	.47	.24	.28	.19	.24	.11	.06
Arithmetic, Gr. 4-6	—.33	.44	.55	.61	.39	.25	.13	.24	.07	.19
English, Gr. 2-3	—.40	.34	.29	.64	.42	.23	.21	.18	—.07	—.03
Fine Arts, Gr. 2-3	—.21	.28	.25	.41	.31	.28	.22	.20	.04	—.07
Fine Arts, Gr. 4-6	—.18	.28	.27	.61	.37	.50	.35	.36	—.09	—.07
Fine Arts, Gr. 7-8	.01	.08	.25	.29	.26	.32	.44	.43	—.04	—.09
History, Gr. 5-6	—.21	.27	.51	.68	.51	.07	.05	.20	.08	.11
History, Gr. 7-8	—.19	.24	.53	.44	.60	.00	.11	.34	.24	.09
Spec. Subjects, Gr. 2-3	—.09	.20	—.02	.26	.05	.45	.24	.12	.15	.03
Deportment, Gr. 2-3	—.19	.25	.07	.32	.17	.53	.36	.35	.04	.01
Deportment, Gr. 4-6	—.08	.17	.17	.41	.35	.61	.42	.51	.05	.02
Deportment, Gr. 7-8	—.11	.23	.15	.28	.25	.44	.46	.70	.01	.00
Effort, Gr. 2-3	—.25	.35	.13	.36	.21	.42	.23	.32	.06	.03
Effort, Gr. 4-6	—.17	.30	.27	.46	.31	.66	.46	.48	.03	.06
Days Present, Gr. 7-8	—.11	—.04	.04	—.07	—.01	.07	.04	—.03	.17	.31

Using the multiple ratio correlation procedure, we find that success in the first year of high school can be predicted to the extent of a correlation of .67 by a composite of these five factors of the grade school record: Average mark in English, grades 4–6; average mark in effort, grades 7–8; average mark in arithmetic, grades 7–8; average days present, grades 4–6; and age at completing the eighth grade. The true weights of these factors, and their approximate weights in terms of class intervals or transmuted scores are given in Table VI. This means that a correlation of .67 with average standing in the first year of high school can be had from composite scores made up in the following manner from five factors of the grade school record, expressed in class intervals: Average score in English, grades 4–6, multiplied by 6; average effort score, grades 7–8, multiplied by 6; average arithmetic score, grades 7–8, multiplied by 4; average days present, grades 4–6, multiplied by −4; and age at completing eighth grade, multiplied by −3. Thus, we find that, whereas an average of the thirty-two factors gives a correlation of .60, five of the thirty-two when combined in this manner will give a correlation of .67.

TABLE VI

The Weights of the Five Most Significant Factors which Enter the Composite for Predicting Success in the First Year of High School

Correlation of Composite with Criterion = .67 $N = 134$

Factor	True β	S.D.	$\dfrac{\text{True } \beta}{\text{S.D.}}$	Approximate Weight
English, Gr. 4–6	1.0000	1.646	.6075	6
Arithmetic, Gr. 7–8	.8863	2.254	.3932	4
Effort, Gr. 7–8	.7884	1.377	.5725	6
Age at End of Gr. 8	—.5008	2.017	—.2483	—3
Days Present, Gr. 4–6	—.3663	1.020	—.3590	—4

Just here a very important question arises: To what extent will this same composite derived for the year 1917 hold true for other years? That is, to what extent does the value of a regression equation of a multiple correlation when obtained from one set of data fluctuate up and down the scale when applied to similar data for other years? In other words, how much dependence can be placed upon such a prediction based upon one situation when applied to another situation? There is a theoretical method employed by statisticians for measuring the reliability of a correlation known as the "P.E. of r," written "P.E.$_r$," the formula of which is, P.E.$_r =$ $.6745 \frac{1-r^2}{\sqrt{N}}$. Table VII shows the P.E.$_r$'s, which correspond to the various values of r and N found in this study. Fortunately, we can also answer this question empirically for the various equations derived. The correlations of this composite with average standing in the first year of high school, when actualy applied to the data for the years 1916, 1918, and 1919, the year preceding and the two years following 1917, are given below:

Year	N	r
1916	102	.68
1917	134	.67
1918	139	.56
1919	137	.65

TABLE VII

P.E.$_r$'s Corresponding to Various Values of r and N

N	Range of r's having the respective P.E.$_r$'s							
	.09	.08	.07	.06	.05	.04	.03	.02
57	.00–.22	.23–.40	.41–.52	.53–.61	.62–.70	.71–.77	.78–.84	.85–.91
90	......	......	.00–.29	.30–.47	.48–.60	.61–.71	.72–.80	.81–.88
102	......	......	.00–.16	.17–.42	.43–.57	.58–.68	.69–.79	.80–.88
134	......	......	......	.00–.23	.24–.47	.48–.63	.64–.75	.76–.86
200	......	......	......	......	.00–.23	.24–.51	.52–.68	.69–.82
386	......	......	......	......	......	......	.00–.52	.53–.75

By referring to Table VII, it will be seen that the size of P.E.$_r$, when r is .67 and N is 134, is .03, which means that the chances are 1 to 1 that the true r lies somewhere between .64 and .70; that is, $\pm$ 1 P.E. The years 1916 and 1919 are within the limits of ± 1 P. E., while the year 1918 is within the limits of ± 4 P.E. For some reason the correlation for the year 1918 is somewhat lower than for the other years. This is true for practically all the correlations of this study and indicates that conditions that year were not entirely normal. It is partially accounted for by the outbreak of the influenza when these pupils were in the first year of high school, for the records show that in a few cases illness and death in the family during that year affected the achievements of pupils whose expected ranks in high school were higher than the actual ones. The superintendent of schools also states that illness made great inroads in the teaching staff during that year.

Notwithstanding this, however, the stability of this equation as indicated by the consistency of the correlations from year to year is remarkable. We can appreciate this all the more when we remember that the correlations of intelligence ratings with success in high school vary all the way from below .30 to around .80, with the central tendency probably somewhere between .45 and .50. Proctor,[1] for example, found the correlation between I. Q.'s obtained on the Stanford-Binet test for one hundred seven pupils and high school marks for one year to be .55, while I. Q.'s obtained on the Army Alpha for four hundred eighty pupils for one year to be .41. Book,[2] in an extensive study involving the pupils of three hundred twenty high schools in Indiana, found the correlation between intelligence ratings and school marks in the junior year of high school to be only .28. His statement in explanation of the relatively low correlation is significant:[3] "It more probably indicates, when taken together with the fact that the correlation between intelligence scores and scholastic success is not very high, that other factors besides intelligence play an important rôle in attaining school success; that we are not, in reality, measuring the same functions; that mere ability to *learn* and *do* are not synonymous with actual performance; that because a pupil has the ability to *learn* or *do* his school work, it by no means follows that he will do it; or that because he has the ability or capacity he can and will properly apply it, when confronted by his tasks in school or life. A mere intelligence test is evidently no criterion for what a pupil will do in school."

It is entirely possible that some of these "other factors," such as, attitude toward the school, habits of indolence or industry, and

[1] Proctor, W. M., *Psychological Tests and Guidance of High School Pupils*, Revised Edition, p. 16, 1923.
[2] Book, W. F., *Intelligence of High School Seniors*, pp. 103, 104, New York, 1922.
[3] *Ibid.*, p. 110.

the like, may be the very things that are taken account of by teachers' marks in the grade school, and, therefore, explain the higher correlations found here. The scatter diagram for the year 1916, with a correlation of .68, is shown in Figure 2.

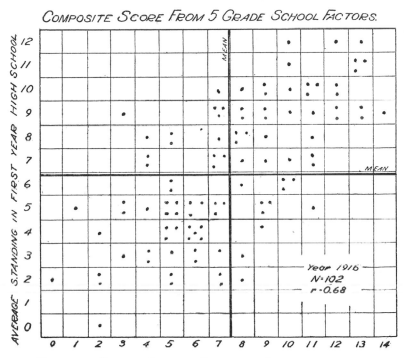

FIGURE 2. SCATTER DIAGRAM SHOWING A CORRELATION OF .68

PREDICTING FIRST YEAR HIGH SCHOOL ENGLISH FROM GRADE SCHOOL RECORD

Having first determined the group of factors which, when combined at the proper weights, would yield a composite score that would correlate to the maximum extent with average standing in the first year of high school, we next sought to find in a similar manner the combination of factors that would best predict the standing in some of the individual subjects in the first year of high school. The first of these was English, a subject which all pupils must take. Table VIII gives the weights of the six factors which enter into the composite giving the maximum correlation with English in the first year of high school, for pupils completing the eighth grade in 1917.

TABLE VIII

WEIGHTS OF THE SIX MOST SIGNIFICANT FACTORS WHICH ENTER THE COMPOSITE FOR PREDICTING ENGLISH RATING IN THE FIRST YEAR OF HIGH SCHOOL

Correlation of Composite with English = .70   N = 134   Year 1917

Factor	True β	S.D.	$\dfrac{\text{True } \beta}{\text{S.D.}}$	Approximate Weight
English, Gr. 4–6............	1.0000	1.646	.6075	6
English, Gr. 7–8............	.9186	1.841	.4990	5
Spec. Subjects, Gr. 4–6......	.7312	1.221	.5988	6
Spec. Subjects, Gr. 7–8......	.5839	1.241	.4705	5
Age, at End of Gr. 8........	—.5438	2.017	—.2696	—3
Grade-Progress.............	.3512	1.226	.2865	3

Again the 1917 equation was applied to the data for the other three years.   The results appear below:

Year	N	r
1916	102	.52
1917	134	.70
1918	139	.61
1919	137	.58

Here a rather surprising thing happened.   The combination which yielded a correlation of .70 for the year 1917, correlated to the extent of only .52 for the year 1916.   Evidently there was something wrong, for we would hardly expect so wide a variation in two successive years.   Since the size of the P.E.$_r$, when r is .70 and N is 134, is only .03, it means that the other correlations are from 3 to 6 P.E.'s away from the 1917 correlation.   Apparently some of the factors which had a close relationship with English success for 1917 did not bear the same relationship for the other years.   Our problem was to

TABLE IX
CORRELATION OF SIX FACTORS WITH ENGLISH IN FIRST YEAR HIGH SCHOOL AND WITH EACH OTHER
Years 1916–1919 N = 102, 134, 139, 137, respectively

	Criterion	English Gr. 4-6	Spec.Sub Gr. 4-6	English Gr. 7-8	Age	Spec. Sub. Gr. 7-8	Grade-Progress
Criterion							
1916		.56	.21	.43	—.37	.19	.10
1917		.54	.47	.53	—.38	.38	.36
1918		.57	.07	.59	—.45	.30	.23
1919		.52	.18	.55	—.22	.13	.31
English 4-6							
1916	.56		.43	.56	—.19	.31	.39
1917	.54		.34	.56	—.33	.25	.30
1918	.57		.35	.65	—.38	.29	.28
1919	.52		.43	.62	—.10	.30	.14
Spec. Subjects 4-6							
1916	.21	.43		.30	—.11	.57	.06
1917	.47	.34		.18	—.12	.48	.27
1918	.07	.35		.30	.13	.49	.42
1919	.18	.43		.28	.24	.43	.07
English 7-8							
1916	.43	.56	.30		—.12	.35	.41
1917	.53	.56	.18		—.30	.18	.23
1918	.59	.65	.30		—.47	.30	.31
1919	.55	.62	.28		—.04	.25	.05
Age							
1916	—.37	—.19	—.11	—.12		.01	—.38
1917	—.38	—.33	—.12	—.30		—.03	—.44
1918	—.45	—.38	.13	—.47		.00	—.57
1919	—.22	—.10	.24	—.04		.01	—.57
Spec. Subjects 7-8							
1916	.19	.31	.57	.35	.01		.03
1917	.38	.25	.48	.18	—.03		.14
1918	.30	.29	.49	.30	.00		—.03
1919	.13	.30	.43	.25	.01		.02
Grade-Progress							
1916	.10	.39	.06	.41	—.38	.03	
1917	.36	.30	.27	.23	—.44	.14	
1918	.23	.28	.42	.31	—.57	—.03	
1919	.31	.14	.07	.05	—.57	.02	
S. D.							
1916	3.33	1.53	1.21	1.69	2.01	1.40	.84
1917	3.09	1.65	1.22	1.84	2.02	1.24	1.23
1918	3.46	1.65	1.19	1.88	1.93	1.39	1.31
1919	3.22	1.57	1.09	2.02	1.64	1.07	1.29
Mean							
1916	7.18	7.83	8.22	7.55	4.18	8.40	4.24
1917	7.36	7.25	8.23	6.82	4.52	8.24	3.78
1918	6.39	7.41	8.09	6.79	4.54	8.24	3.53
1919	7.16	7.26	7.93	6.79	4.18	8.46	3.39

discover, therefore, which of these factors were consistent and which were not. To do this the correlation with the criterion of each of the six factors found significant for the year 1917 was obtained for each of the years separately, and likewise the several intercorrelations. These appear in Table IX.

Table IX clearly shows that three of the factors, English 4–6, English 7–8, and age, are remarkably consistent, both as regards the criterion correlations and the several intercorrelations, and a fourth factor, special subjects 7–8, is fairly consistent, while two factors, special subjects 4–6 and grade-progress, are very inconsistent. The criterion correlations of special subjects 4–6 vary from .47 to .07, and those of grade-progress vary from .36 to .10. Apparently, the relatively high correlations of these factors for the year 1917 were merely accidental. In order to secure a more accurate measure of their true significance, the relative weights of the six factors were determined for the year 1918 in the same manner as was done for the year 1917. These new weights for the year 1918 are given in Table X.

A comparison of Table X with Table VIII, the corresponding table for 1917, is instructive. While the correlation for the two years remains practically identical, .69 for 1918 as against .70 for

TABLE X

The Weights of the Six Most Significant Factors which Enter the Composite for Predicting English Rating in the First Year of High School

Correlation of Composite with Criterion = .69 N = .139   Year 1918

Factor	True β	S. D.	$\dfrac{\text{True } \beta}{\text{S. D.}}$	Approximate Weight
English, Gr. 4–6	1.0000	1.648	.6067	10
English, Gr. 7–8	1.1831	1.876	.6307	10
Age at End Gr. 8	—.7142	1.931	—.3699	—6
Spec. Subjects, Gr. 7–8	.5311	1.388	.3826	6
Spec. Subjects, Gr. 4–6	—.6080	1.193	—.5096	—8
Grade-Progress	—.1886	1.305	—.1442	—2

1917, the relative weights of the factors entering into the composites have shifted materially for the factors, special subjects 4–6 and grade-progress, while they remain fairly constant for the other factors. This seems to verify our hypothesis that the correlations of these factors for the year 1917 were merely accidental. Certainly, it would seem unwise to permit factors to enter into the composite whose true β weight varies in two successive years from .7312 to —.6080 in the one case, and from .3512 to —.1886 in the other. The relative weights of the other four factors are not greatly altered from those of 1917, which indicates that their relationship to success in English is real and not spurious. The correlations of the new composite of four factors is given below for each of the years:

Year	N	r
1916	102	.60
1917	134	.67
1918	139	.67
1919	137	.60

It was the writer's original purpose to find the best compromise weights for the several factors for the years 1917 and 1918, and then apply these weights to the other two years. However, the weights for the four significant factors for the two years were so similar as to make this unnecessary, the new weights producing a correlation of .67 in both cases. These results suggest a possible explanation of inconsistencies which sometimes appear in multiple equations made up from the results of a single group when applied to a new situation, and the technique followed here may point the way out of the difficulty. Certainly, if these fluctuations are due to the variations in the correlations of some of the factors in the multiple regression equation, this procedure will reveal it. In the same way it will enable one to build up a reliable equation that is based upon a larger and more representative sampling than is possible by the usual procedure. Here, for example, basing regression equation on four successive years amounts to practically the same thing as quadrupling N.

It remains now to show how these correlations compare with those obtained from standard tests. Book[1] reports a correlation of .44 between group intelligence ratings and average English marks

[1] Book, *op. cit.*, p. 105.

for one high school in Indianapolis. Proctor[1] found that the correlation between Test No. 9, in Army Scale, Group Examinations *a* and *b*, and English marks made by 171 pupils in the first year of high school was .48. These are typical cases. It is clear, therefore, that the correlations obtained between grade school composites and first year high school are considerably higher than intelligence tests yield.

PREDICTING FIRST YEAR LATIN FROM GRADE SCHOOL RECORD

The weights of the seven factors which enter into the composite which best predicts first year Latin are given in Table XI. The correlation for the year 1917 is .73. The magnitude of the correlations when this equation was applied to the other four years appears below:

Year	N	r
1916	51	.58
1917	57	.73
1918	58	.57
1919	62	.64

It is possible that slightly different weights for the factors might have produced a somewhat more consistent correlation. Time

TABLE XI

WEIGHTS OF THE SEVEN MOST SIGNIFICANT FACTORS WHICH ENTER THE COMPOSITE FOR PREDICTING FIRST YEAR LATIN

Correlation of Composite with Criterion = .73   N = 57

Factor	True β	S. D.	$\dfrac{\text{True } \beta}{\text{S. D.}}$	Approximate Weight
English, Gr. 7–8	1.0000	1.728	.5787	10
Arithmetic, Gr. 7–8	.5135	2.214	.2319	4
History, Gr. 5–6	.9397	1.530	.6142	10
Age at End Gr. 8	—.4904	1.757	—.2791	—5
Days Present, Gr. 4–6	—.5786	1.123	—.5152	—9
Days Present, Gr. 2–3	—.4029	1.311	—.3073	—5
Grade-Progress	.4531	1.060	.4275	7

[1] Proctor, *op. cit.*, p. 40.

did not permit, however, the carrying out of the procedure employed in stabilizing the equation used in the case of English. As it is, the correlations are sufficiently high to be of service in predicting success in a subject where such an instrument is especially needed because of the high mortality. Allen,[1] for example, found that his six best tests when combined into a multiple yielded a correlation of .59 for the first semester of Latin, but this correlation dropped to .48 for the second semester.

PREDICTING FIRST YEAR HIGH SCHOOL MATHEMATICS FROM THE GRADE SCHOOL RECORD

It was not possible to discover any combination of grade school factors that would correlate very highly with first year high school mathematics. The five factors found most significant for this purpose appear in Table XII. The correlation of this composite with first year mathematics for each of the four years is given below:

Year	N	r
1916	101	.42
1917	134	.51
1918	141	.43
1919	137	.51

While these correlations are fairly consistent from year to year, they are in every case considerably lower than those we found for

TABLE XII

WEIGHTS OF THE FIVE MOST SIGNIFICANT FACTORS WHICH ENTER INTO THE COMPOSITE FOR PREDICTING SUCCESS IN THE FIRST YEAR HIGH SCHOOL MATHEMATICS

Correlation of Composite with Criterion = .51   N = 134

Factor	True β	S.D.	$\dfrac{\text{True } \beta}{\text{S.D.}}$	Approximate Weight
Arithmetic, Gr. 7–8	1.0000	2.254	.4437	9
English, Gr. 4–6	.5579	1.646	.3389	7
Spec. Subjects, Gr. 7–8	—.4425	1.241	—.3566	—7
Grade-Progress	.3094	1.226	.2524	5
Days Present, Gr. 2–3	.3338	1.347	.2478	5

[1] Allen, *op. cit.*, p. 32.

English and Latin, but they are in substantial agreement with the results of other investigators who have found only slight relationship between algebra ability and standing in other subjects. Proctor, for example, found high school algebra and I. Q.'s obtained on Stanford-Binet test for 113 cases to be .46.[1] Any adequate scheme for sectioning pupils in mathematics in the first year of high school will necessitate the development of special tests for diagnosing potential mathematical ability, which seems to be very specific in character.

PREDICTING AVERAGE ACHIEVEMENT OF PUPILS WHO
REMAIN TWO OR MORE YEARS IN HIGH SCHOOL

In addition to seeking the composite of grade school factors which would best predict success in the first year of high school, the writer attempted to discover the factors which would yield the maximum prediction of average standing in all subjects, and average standing in English, for all pupils who remained in high school for two years or more. Of the 134 pupils of the 1917 class who were in high school at the end of the first year, 90 continued for at least one more year, and of these 71 continued in school till graduation. The six grade school factors which yield the maximum correlation with average success in high school for pupils remaining two or more years appear in Table XIII. The correlation of this composite with each of the four years is given below:

Year	N	r
1916	70	.60
1917	90	.64
1918	106	.57
1919	116	.66

A comparison of these results with similar correlations with first year high school success reveal two interesting facts. First, it will be noted that in general these correlations are slightly lower than the corresponding correlations for first year high school, here being .60, .64, .57, and .66, for the four years, respectively, as against .68, .67, .56 and .65 in the former case. One fact which has contributed to this has been the reduced range of the pupils remaining in high school. A point of greater interest, however, is the fact that the five factors predicting first year high school success,

[1] Proctor, *op. cit.*, p. 38.

and the six factors best predicting high school success over the longer period, are almost identical, grade-progress in the latter case replacing days present, grades 4–6, in the former, English, grades 7–8, being added, and the other factors remaining unchanged. In fact, when the former equation was applied to see to what extent it would predict average standing for two or more years, the following results were obtained: For 1916, .62; for 1917, .60; for 1918, .57; and for 1919, .66. These correlations are almost identical with the corresponding correlations obtained with the new equation, and it indicates clearly that not only do the same factors that contribute to high school success in the first year contribute to success throughout the high school period, but that their relative importance continues substantially the same. The magnitude of these correlations compares favorably with that of .49, between I. Q.'s obtained on the Stanford-Binet scale and average of all marks in the high school for two and one-half years, as reported by Proctor.[1] The corresponding correlation between the I. Q.'s and average marks for one year in high school was .55. Book[2] obtained a correlation of .47 between intelligence scores and average scholastic success during the entire high school period, and Terman[3] reports a correlation of .45 between mental age and average marks in the high school.

TABLE XIII

WEIGHTS OF THE SIX FACTORS WHICH ENTER INTO THE COMPOSITE FOR PREDICTING AVERAGE ACHIEVEMENT OF PUPILS WHO REMAIN TWO OR MORE YEARS IN HIGH SCHOOL

Correlation of Composite with Criterion = .64 N = 90

Factor	True β	S.D.	$\dfrac{\text{True } \beta}{\text{S.D.}}$	Approximate Weight
Arithmetic, Gr. 7–8	1.0000	2.283	.4380	9
English, Gr. 4–6	.7515	1.633	.4602	9
Grade-Progress	.5255	1.174	.4476	9
English, Gr. 7–8	.6447	1.893	.3406	7
Effort, Gr. 7–8	.3903	1.464	.2666	5
Age at End Gr. 8	—.2880	1.664	—.1731	—3

[1] Proctor, *op. cit.*, p. 16.
[2] Book, *op. cit.*, p. 105.
[3] Terman, L. M., *The Intelligence of School Children*, p. 79, Boston, 1919.

In a similar manner the four factors that, when combined, best predict average standing in English for pupils who remain in the high school for two years or longer, were determined. These factors appear in Table XIV. Here it is seen that three of these factors are the same that entered into the composite for predicting success in English in the first year of high school, but history, grades 7–8, has replaced age for the fourth factor. The correlation of this composite with each of the years is as follows:

Year	N	r
1916	70	.62
1917	90	.67
1918	106	.52
1919	116	.60

The corresponding correlations for the first year high school English for the four years are, respectively, .60, .67, .67, and .60, and, except for the year 1918, which persists in showing erratic tendencies, the later correlations are substantially the same. We may say again, therefore, that, in general, the same factors which contribute to a pupil's success in the first year high school English, determine his English standing for the entire high school period.

TABLE XIV

WEIGHTS OF THE FOUR FACTORS ENTERING INTO THE COMPOSITE FOR
PREDICTING AVERAGE STANDING IN ENGLISH FOR ALL PUPILS
WHO REMAIN TWO OR MORE YEARS IN HIGH SCHOOL

Correlation of Composite with Criterion = .67   N = 90

Factor	True β	S. D.	$\dfrac{\text{True }\beta}{\text{S. D.}}$	Approximate Weight
English, Gr. 4–6	1.0000	1.663	.6013	10
History, Gr. 7–8	.7504	1.695	.4427	7
English, Gr. 7–8	.6984	1.893	.3689	6
Spec. Subjects, Gr. 7–8	.5430	1.327	.4092	7

HOW THESE RESULTS APPLY TO ANOTHER CITY

That multiple correlation formulas derived from the data of one year show but slight fluctuations when applied to similar data for other years *in the same situation* now seems to be demonstrated.

One further test still remains: How stable will these equations be when applied to similar data but for another city, where conditions are wholly different? This question is a crucial one. A practical school administrator might think something like this: "These relations might be true enough in New Rochelle, New York, but how would they work in *my city* where things are entirely different?" Realizing this the writer subjected these regression equations to another rigid test. He applied the equations for predicting first year high school success, as derived in New Rochelle, New York, for the year 1917, to the pupils who entered West High School in Des Moines, Iowa, from eight elementary schools in the fall of 1922. These were the last pupils for whom a year's records were available, one hundred twenty in all. For purposes of comparison these results are given in Table XV, together with the corresponding results for the four years in New Rochelle, New York.

TABLE XV

CORRELATION OF GRADE SCHOOL COMPOSITE SCORES WITH GENERAL AVERAGE, ENGLISH, LATIN, AND MATHEMATICS IN FIRST YEAR OF HIGH SCHOOL, FOR FOUR SUCCESSIVE YEARS IN NEW ROCHELLE, NEW YORK, AND FOR ONE YEAR IN DES MOINES, IOWA

Grade School Composite	New Rochelle, New York				Des Moines, Iowa
	1916	1917	1918	1919	1922
General Average	.68	.67	.56	.65	.69
English	.60	.67	.67	.60	.61
Latin	.58	.73	.57	.64	.61
Mathematics	.42	.51	.43	.51	.51

When an equation for four years in one situation and for a group five years later in a totally different situation fluctuated only between .56 and .69, as is done in the case of the General Average, or only between .60 and .67, as is done in the case of English, its consistency must be considered little less than remarkable. The equations for Latin and mathematics are almost as stable. When we remember that intelligence test scores and high school marks fluctuate between about .30 as found by Book, and some investigators, to around .70 as found by other investigators, this consistency is all the more surprising.

It would be hard to get two cities more unlike than New Rochelle and Des Moines, one a wealthy residential city just out of New York City and the other a rich industrial and trading center in the heart of the Middle West. Certainly, relationships that hold true under such widely dissimilar conditions cannot be considered accidental. No multiple correlation formulas which the writer has been able to find have ever been subjected to such a rigid test, and no correlations of any kind have ever shown more consistent agreement.

A COMPARISON OF GRADE SCHOOL COMPOSITES AND STANDARD TESTS

In a few cases it has been found possible to compare these results in New Rochelle with similar correlations between standard tests and high school achievement in other school situations, but no direct comparisons have been found possible, as such tests were little used prior to 1917. However, 79 of the 120 pupils entering high school in the fall of 1922 in Des Moines had taken three standard tests in the April preceding. These tests were the Terman Group Intelligence Test, Thorndike-McCall Reading Test and Woody-McCall Mixed Fundamentals in Arithmetic. The comparison of the correlation between these test scores and the four criteria of first year high school success, and corresponding correlations between grade school composite scores and these same criteria, is given in Table XVI.

TABLE XVI

CORRELATION OF ACHIEVEMENT IN FIRST YEAR HIGH SCHOOL
WITH GRADE SCHOOL COMPOSITE SCORES, INTELLIGENCE,
READING AND ARITHMETIC TEST SCORES

Factor	General Average	English	Latin	Mathematics
Grade School Composite*	.63	.61	.58	.55
Terman Intelligence Test	.37	.46	.18	.42
Thorndike-McCall Reading Test	.33	.33	.48	.31
Woody-McCall Arithmetic Test	.40	.34	.44	.46

)

* The variations in the size of the correlations of the grade school composites with the four criteria of high school success from the same correlations for the larger group of 120, as given in Table XV, are due to the influence upon the smaller group of a few scattering cases, who had taken the tests in some instances but not in others.

In every case the correlations with the composite scores are somewhat higher than are the corresponding correlations with the test scores, and in the case of the General Average they are markedly higher, .63, as against .37 for Terman, .33 for Thorndike-McCall, and .40 for Woody-McCall. This, of course, does not mean that standard tests are worthless instruments for predicting academic success in the first year of high school, nor, indeed, that they are, under ordinary circumstances, necessarily inferior to composite scores made up from the grade school record, for it will be noted that the particular tests available here happen to be extremely brief and the number of cases is entirely too few to warrant any claim to finality. However, it does indicate that standard tests alone may sometimes prove inadequate, and it emphasizes the fact that educational psychologists have hitherto given too little attention to one of the most promising sources of data needed for predicting high school success, namely, the records of the pupils in the grades. Moreover, it suggests that what is probably needed is not merely intelligence tests, which afford measures of native ability, nor achievement tests, which provide definite objective comparisons of the prerequisite academic knowledge, nor teachers' ratings in the grades, which reflect, in some degree at least, the habits of study and moral attributes of the pupils already acquired,—none of these alone; but that rather what is needed is a proper combination of all three weighted according to their respective importance as instruments of prediction. Evidence in support of this conclusion is afforded by the fact that such combinations as can be made from the three brief tests here available and the grade school record raise the correlations with first year high school success yielded by the grade school composites alone, as follows: General Average, from .63 to .69; English, from .61 to .68; Latin, from .58 to .73; and mathematics, from .55 to .65. This increase is made possible by the relatively low correlations of the three tests with each other and with the grade school composites, a fact which indicates that they do not all measure the same things and so may supplement each other (see Table XVII).

WHAT DO THESE CORRELATIONS MEAN?

To any person other than a trained statistician the statement that a correlation is .70 or .60, for example, means very little. To say that it is "high," "marked," or "significant" is still to leave

TABLE XVII

CORRELATIONS OF THREE STANDARD TESTS WITH GRADE SCHOOL
COMPOSITES AND WITH EACH OTHER

Test	With Grade School Composites				With Tests		
	General Average	English	Latin	Mathematics	Terman	Th'ndike-McCall	Woody-McCall
Terman............	.33	.32	.21	.31	..	.36	.40
Thorndike–McCall ..	.42	.45	.45	.39	.36	..	.12
Woody–McCall	.25	.29	.16	.34	.40	.12	..

its meaning vague and unsatisfactory. Therefore a question of great practical importance is: In perfectly understandable terms, what does a correlation of .70 or .60 actually mean? It is hoped that Tables XVIII and XIX may throw some light on this question. These tables are based upon original tables compiled by Professor E. L. Thorndike, by whose permission they are included here. Table XVIII shows the percentage distribution of successive quintiles and Table XIX shows what these percentages would mean, assuming that one has a group of two hundred pupils to be divided into five sections. Table XVIII means that on an average, of the highest and lowest fifth of the pupils in the test, when r is .70, 56.5 per cent will be exactly placed, 25.9 per cent in the group adjacent, 12.2 per cent will fall in the next group, 4.6 per cent in the next group and .8 per cent in the group farthest away. Likewise,

TABLE XVIII

APPROXIMATE PERCENTAGE DISTRIBUTION OF SUCCESSIVE QUINTILES
OF THE GROUP IN ACHIEVEMENT, CORRESPONDING TO THE
SUCCESSIVE QUINTILES ON THE TEST. WHEN r = .70,
AND WHEN r = .60

Quintiles on Test	Corresponding Quintiles in Achievement (r = .70)					Quintiles on Test	Corresponding Quintiles in Achievement (r = .60)				
	First	Second	Third	Fourth	Fifth		First	Second	Third	Fourth	Fifth
Fifth....	.8	4.6	12.2	25.9	56.5	Fifth....	2.3	7.5	14.8	26.0	49.4
Fourth..	4.6	14.7	24.1	30.7	25.9	Fourth..	7.5	16.2	22.8	27.5	26.0
Third...	12.2	24.1	27.4	24.1	12.2	Third...	14.8	22.8	24.8	22.8	14.8
Second..	25.9	30.7	24.1	14.7	4.6	Second..	26.0	27.5	22.8	16.2	7.5
First....	56.5	25.9	12.2	4.6	.8	First....	49.4	26.0	14.8	7.5	2.3

when *r* is .60, 49.4 per cent will be exactly placed, 26 per cent will fall in the adjacent group, 14.8 per cent will fall in the next group, 7.5 per cent in the next, and 2.3 per cent in the group farthest away. What these percentages would mean if one had 200 pupils and divided them into five equal groups on the basis of the tests is given in Table XIX. Here we see that the 40 pupils in the highest group according to the test and the 40 pupils in the lowest group according to the test would be in groups on the basis of achievement as follows: When *r* equals .70, 23 pupils are placed exactly, 10 pupils in the group adjacent, 5 pupils in the next group, and 2 pupils in the next; when *r* equals .60, 20 pupils are exactly placed, 10 pupils in the group adjacent, etc. In the same manner these tables show the distribution for the other three groups. It seems, therefore, that one may expect 4 out of 5 pupils to be placed either in the exact fifths in achievement or the groups adjacent, when *r* equals .70, and the 3 out of 4 will be placed either in the exact fifths in achievement or the adjacent groups, when *r* equals .60. Or, stated in another way, when correlations lie between .60 and .70, as most of those in the present study do, from 25 to 56 per cent are placed by the tests in the exact fifth where they belong, as against 20 per cent by chance, and only from 5 to 10 per cent are displaced by as much as three groups, whereas from 20 to 40 per cent would be so displaced by chance groupings.

TABLE XIX

AVERAGE DISTRIBUTION OF 200 CASES IN ACHIEVEMENT WHEN SEPARATED INTO FIVE EQUAL GROUPS ACCORDING TO QUINTILE RATING ON THE TEST. WHEN *r* = .70, AND WHEN *r* = .60

Quintiles on Test	Corresponding Quintiles in Achievement (*r* = .70)					Quintiles on Test	Corresponding Quintiles in Achievement (*r* = .60)				
	First	Second	Third	Fourth	Fifth		First	Second	Third	Fourth	Fifth
Fifth....	..	2	5	10	23	Fifth....	1	3	6	10	20
Fourth..	2	6	10	12	10	Fourth..	3	7	9	11	10
Third...	5	10	10	10	5	Third...	6	9	10	9	6
Second..	10	12	10	6	2	Second..	10	11	9	7	3
First....	23	10	5	2	..	First....	20	10	6	3	1

Now let us see how these theoretical groupings compare with the actual groupings found in the present study. If the pupils entering high school for each of the five years studied had been separated into four groups on the basis of the composite scores of the significant grade school factors, to what extent would these groupings correspond with four groups made on the basis of actual achievement in the first year of high school? Table XX shows the amount of quartile displacement from the expected positions of the lowest and highest quartiles for each of the groups studied. Let us take the first item

TABLE XX

ACTUAL DISTRIBUTION ON BASIS OF FIRST YEAR HIGH SCHOOL
ACHIEVEMENT CORRESPONDING TO THE HIGHEST AND LOWEST
QUARTILES ON BASIS OF THE COMPOSITE SCORES

General Average, English, Mathematics, and Latin, for the Years 1916,
1917, 1918, 1919, in New Rochelle, New York; and for the
Year 1922 in Des Moines, Iowa

Group	Lowest Quartile Distribution				Highest Quartile Distribution			
	Q_1	Q_2	Q_3	Q_4	Q_1	Q_2	Q_3	Q_4
GENERAL AVERAGE								
N. R.,* 1916	14	7	4	..	..	1	4	20
1917	20	10	3	..	..	1	7	25
1918	22	8	6	1	3	4	7	23
1919	20	7	5	1	..	6	7	20
Total	76	32	18	2	3	12	25	88
Per cent	59.4	25.0	14.0	1.6	2.3	9.4	19.5	68.8
N. R. (4-yr. Ave.)	18	8	4	..	1	3	6	20
D. M.,† 1922	20	8	1	1	1	3	7	19
Per cent	66.7	26.7	3.3	3.3	3.3	10.0	23.4	63.3
ENGLISH								
N. R., 1916	14	6	3	2	..	5	7	13
1917	23	8	2	1	..	3	12	19
1918	23	9	2	1	2	1	10	22
1919	27	3	4	..	1	5	10	18
Total	87	26	11	4	3	14	39	72
Per cent	68.0	20.3	8.6	3.1	2.3	10.9	30.5	56.3
N. R. (4-yr. Ave.)	20	6	3	1	1	3	9	17
D. M., 1922	20	8	2	..	1	5	5	19
Per cent	66.7	26.7	6.6	..	3.3	16.7	16.7	63.3

* N. R. = New Rochelle.
† D. M. = Des Moines.

TABLE XX (Continued)

Group	Lowest Quartile Distribution				Highest Quartile Distribution			
	Q₁	Q₂	Q₃	Q₄	Q₁	Q₂	Q₃	Q₄
MATHEMATICS								
N. R., 1916	11	8	4	2	..	2	6	17
1917	16	11	5	1	1	5	7	20
1918	16	11	6	2	1	6	7	21
1919	19	8	5	2	1	5	9	19
Total	62	38	20	7	3	18	29	77
Per cent	48.0	30.0	15.7	5.5	2.4	14.2	22.8	60.6
N. R. (4-yr. Ave.)	13	8	5	2	1	4	6	17
D. M., 1922	17	7	2	2	2	2	10	14
Per cent	60.6	25.0	7.2	7.2	7.2	7.2	35.6	50.0
LATIN								
N. R., 1916	8	4	1	..	..	2	6	5
1917	10	3	..	1	..	2	4	8
1918	10	4	..	..	..	1	6	7
1919	7	7	1	..	..	..	3	12
Total	35	18	2	1		5	19	32
Per cent	62.5	32.1	3.6	1.8	..	8.5	34.0	57.5
N. R. (4-yr. Ave.)	13	6	1	..	..	2	7	11
D. M., 1922	11	6	3	..	1	1	8	10
Per cent	55.0	30.0	15.0	..	5.0	5.0	40.0	50.0

in the table, for example. In 1916 there were 25 pupils whom we would expect, on basis of composite scores, to be in the lowest quartile in average standing in the first year of high school, but as a matter of fact, 14 of these pupils are in the lowest quartile, 7 are in the next quartile, and 4 are in the next. In the same way, of the 25 pupils whom we would expect, on basis of composite scores, to be in the highest quartile, 20 pupils are really in the highest quartile, 4 are in the next quartile, and 1 in the next. Figure 3 shows graphically the actual distribution, on the basis of first year high school achievement, corresponding to the highest and lowest quartiles on the basis of the composite scores for the Des Moines group and for a group of the same size at New Rochelle with the average percentage distribution of the four years. In this figure each + represents a pupil whose expected position is in the highest

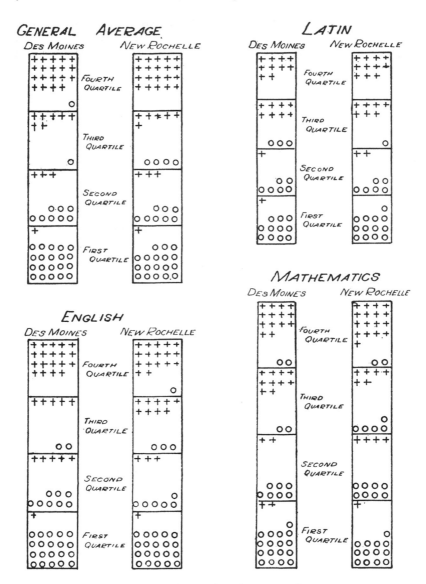

FIGURE 3. ACTUAL DISTRIBUTION OF UPPER AND LOWER QUARTILES
IN HIGH SCHOOL ACHIEVEMENT CORRESPONDING TO EXPECTED
DISTRIBUTIONS

(See page 41 for explanation.)

quartile, and each O represents a pupil whose expected position is in the lowest quartile. The actual quartile position of these pupils on the basis of first year high school achievement is shown by the position on the chart.

SUMMARY AND CONCLUSIONS

1. The factors of the grade school record vary widely in their relation to high school success. The correlations with average standing in the first year of high school range from —.36 to .56; with English the range is from — .38 to .54; with Latin the range is from — .26 to .42.

2. These factors when combined by the multiple ratio correlation method will give predictions of first year high school success that are both significant and consistent. For four successive years, the correlations with average standing in first year high school are, respectively, .68, .67, .56, .65; with English the correlations are, respectively, .60,.67, .67, .60; with Latin the correlations are .58, .73, .57, .64; and with mathematics the correlations are .42, .51, .43, .51.

3. The most important factors in relation to high school success are as follows: Age at completing grade 8; grade-progress; English, grades 4–6; English, grades 7–8; arithmetic, grades 7–8; special subjects, grades 7–8; history, grades 5–6; history, grades 7–8; effort, grades 7–8; days present, grades 2–3; and days present, grades 4–6. The relative importance of these factors varies with different high school subjects.

4. The correlations between composite scores obtained from grade school factors and average standing of pupils who remain in high school two or more years are .60, .64, .57, .66, respectively, for the years 1916, 1917, 1918, 1919, in one city. Similarly, the correlations with average standing in English are, respectively, .62, .67, .52, .60. In general, the same factors that predict success in the first year of high school will predict success during the whole high school period, and to substantially the same extent.

5. Regression equations derived from the data in one situation show remarkable consistency when applied to a wholly new situation five years later.

6. The correlations between composites of grade school factors and high school success are high enough to be of practical signi-

ficance, placing, as they do, from 70 to 82 per cent of the pupils in the exact or adjacent fifths. This is considerably better than that afforded by standard tests and at the same time they are more consistent from year to year.

7. The best basis for predicting high school success would seem to be a combination of the following: Intelligence ratings, to afford some measure of native endowment; standard achievement tests, to give objective evidence as to prerequisite academic preparation; and teachers' ratings in the grades, to afford a measure of the attitudes and moral habits already acquired, which are such important factors in determining high school success.

CHAPTER IV

RELATION BETWEEN GRADE SCHOOL RECORD AND PERSISTENCE IN HIGH SCHOOL

WHO GRADUATES FROM OUR HIGH SCHOOLS?

What type of pupils are those who finish the eighth grade and then do not enter high school? What type of pupils compose that large group which enter high school but fall out during or at the end of the first year of high school? What type of pupils remain in high school longer than one year, but drop out before graduating? What type of pupils graduate from high school? These are questions of great significance to school officials and of interest to the public generally. If it were possible to know in advance these four types of pupils, the problem of guidance would be greatly simplified and this information would be of much value to administrative officers in determining budgetary allowances. Moreover, it would be the first step in isolating the influence of each of the factors that determine whether or not a pupil is to go to high school and if so how long.

The writer attempted to find out to what extent the grade school record of these four groups differed. To do this it was necessary to know whether or not a pupil entered any high school after completing grade 8, and if so, how long he remained. It was comparatively easy to secure this information for those pupils entering the New Rochelle High School, as the cards would indicate length of stay there and in most cases whether or not the pupils transferred to another school. These pupils could then be traced by letter.

Two groups of pupils, however, presented special difficulty: those who did not enter New Rochelle High School, and those whose records did not indicate cause of leaving. The high school principal and teachers were consulted about those who dropped out of high school. Grade school principal and teachers often knew about those pupils as well as about many who had not entered high school. If the families still lived in New Rochelle they were reached by telephone or letter, or, failing in that, by personal visit. Fortunately,

New Rochelle has a fairly stable population. Usually some neighbor could tell us about families who had moved away. These could then be reached by letter. For the year 1917 the schools outside New Rochelle which these pupils were reported to have attended were written, and in only one case was there an error and this of little consequence. One pupil was said to have graduated from a Southern high school, but it was found he had really dropped out in the fourth year. It is therefore felt that this information is trustworthy and represents actual statistics of elimination. The writer had to drop fewer than one per cent of all pupils completing grade 8 for the four years because of inability to trace them till high school graduation or till actually quitting school. OBrien[1] took no account of pupils transferring to other schools; nor apparently has any one else who has investigated elimination from high schools. And yet this group, often a large one, must affect the percentage who *actually* drop out at the various stages of high school, as distinguished from those who merely drop out of some one particular school.

Table XXI shows distribution of eighth grade pupils of New Rochelle for the years 1916, 1917, 1918, 1919, according to length

TABLE XXI

DISTRIBUTION OF PUPILS ON BASIS OF LENGTH OF STAY IN
HIGH SCHOOL

Group	1916			1917			1918			1919			Total 1916–1919		
	Boys	Girls	Total	Boys	Girls	Total	Boys	Girls	Total	Boys	Girls	Total	Boys	Girls	Total
High School Graduates	34	23	57	36	35	71	45	33	78	55	55	110	170	146	316
Non-Graduates, Over One Year High School	10	22	32	16	20	36	21	38	59	13	18	31	60	98	158
Non-Graduates, One Year High School	16	14	30	29	22	51	13	14	27	10	13	23	68	63	131
Pupils Who Do Not Enter High School	13	9	22	28	14	42	25	25	50	14	16	30	80	64	144
Total Completing Grade 8	73	68	141	109	91	200	104	110	214	92	102	194	377	372	749

[1] OBrien, F. J., *The High School Failures*, Teachers College, Columbia University, Contributions to Education, No. 102, p. 5, New York, 1919.

TABLE XXII

PERCENTAGE DISTRIBUTION ON BASIS OF LENGTH OF STAY IN
HIGH SCHOOL

Group	1916			1917			1918			1919			Total 1916–1919		
	Boys	Girls	Total	Boys	Girls	Total	Boys	Girls	Total	Boys	Girls	Total	Boys	Girls	Total
High School Graduates	46.6	33.8	40.4	33.0	38.4	35.5	43.3	30.0	36.5	59.8	53.9	56.7	45.1	39.3	42.2
Non-Graduates, Over One Year High School	13.7	32.3	22.7	14.7	22.0	18.0	20.2	34.6	27.6	14.1	17.6	16.0	15.7	26.6	21.1
Non-Graduates, One Year High School	21.9	20.6	21.3	26.6	24.2	25.5	12.5	12.7	12.6	10.9	12.8	11.8	18.0	16.0	17.5
Pupils Who Do Not Enter High School	17.8	13.3	15.6	25.7	15.4	21.0	24.0	22.7	23.3	15.2	15.7	15.5	21.2	17.2	19.2

of stay in high school. Table XXII gives these distributions expressed in percentages and makes comparisons easier.

It will be noted that the percentage of boys graduating varies from 33.0 to 59.8. The percentage of girls graduating varies from 30.0 to 53.9. The percentage of boys not entering high school varies from 15.2 to 25.7. The percentage of girls not entering varies from 13.3 to 22.7. The percentage of boys remaining in high school one year or less varies from 10.9 to 26.6. The percentage of girls remaining in high school one year or less varies from 12.7 to 24.2. The differences between the sexes are very slight. This is entirely in accord with OBrien[1] who says: "Nowhere is there any definite indication that any of the prognosis (of high school failures) operates more distinctly or more pronouncedly on either boys or girls."

In this study boys and girls were treated separately in regard to age, where again no significant differences were found. Since these findings are in agreement with other studies, none of which have found significant sex differences, during the remainder of this study boys and girls have been treated together.

In comparing the records of the pupils who graduate from high school with those of the pupils who do not enter the high school at all, with those of the pupils who enter the high school but remain

[1] OBrien, *op. cit.*, p. 45.

one year or less, and with those of the pupils who remain in high school longer than one year but do not graduate, two measures of the differences between the groups have been used. In the first place the differences between the means of the graduating group and the means of each of the other three groups, together with the reliability of these differences, have been secured for the various school subjects in the grade school, and for effort, deportment, and attendance. In the second place, the percentage of each of the three groups which equals or exceeds the median of the graduating group has been calculated for age at completing grade 8, grade-progress, attendance, and average marks in the grade school subjects, effort, and deportment. These comparisons have been made for each of the four years separately.

AGE AS A FACTOR IN DETERMINING PERSISTENCE

What relation does the age at which a pupil finishes grade 8 bear to persistence in high school? OBrien[1] found that the percentage of pupils graduating from high school who entered at the

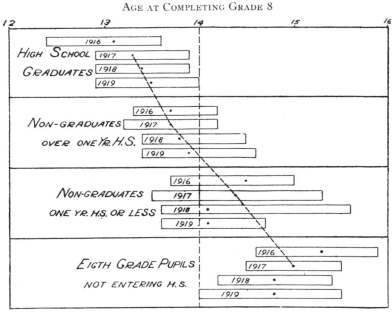

FIGURE 4.   AGE DISTRIBUTION OF MIDDLE 50 PER CENT OF PUPILS ON BASIS OF LENGTH OF STAY IN HIGH SCHOOL

[1] OBrien, *op. cit.*, p. 34.

age of twelve is approximately four times that of the pupils who enter at the age of seventeen. It is the conclusion of Van Denburg[2] from his study of one thousand pupils in the high schools of New York City that "on the whole the economic status of these pupils seems to be only a slight factor in the determination of length of stay in high school," and he puts "late entering age" at the head of the list of factors favoring elimination from high school. Figure 4 shows the overlappings of the middle fifty per cent of each of the four groups for the years 1916, 1917, 1918, and 1919, separately. Of those who graduate from high school the median age at completing grade 8 ranges from 13.1 to 13.5 years; of those who remain in high school over one year but do not graduate, the median age ranges from 13.7 to 13.9 years, of those who stay in high school one year or less, the median age ranges from 14.1 to 14.5 years; and of

TABLE XXIII

DISTRIBUTION OF HIGH SCHOOL PUPILS SHOWING RELATION OF
AGE TO PERSISTENCE IN HIGH SCHOOL

Number and Percentage of Pupils of Each Group Equaling or Exceeding
Various Ages at Time of Completing Grade 8

Age	Completing Grade Eight		Not Entering High School		High School Entrants							
					One Year		Over One Year		Graduates		Total	
	N	Per cent	N	Per cent	N	Per cent	N	Per cent	N	Per cent	N	Per cent
11	2	100.0							2	100.0	2	100.0
11½	5	99.7							5	99.4	5	99.6
12	22	99.0					1	100.0	21	97.8	22	98.7
12½	55	96.1			3	100.0	10	99.4	42	91.2	55	95.1
13	112	88.8	4	100.0	11	97.8	22	93.1	75	77.9	108	86.0
13½	159	73.8	9	97.2	28	89.4	44	79.1	78	54.2	150	68.1
14	132	52.6	21	91.0	23	68.0	34	51.3	54	29.5	111	43.3
14½	92	35.0	28	76.4	23	50.4	18	29.8	23	12.4	64	25.1
15	70	22.7	33	56.9	13	32.8	12	18.4	12	5.1	37	14.5
15½	58	13.4	27	34.0	16	22.9	14	10.8	1	1.3	31	8.4
16	22	4.6	13	15.3	4	10.6	3	1.9	2	1.0	9	3.3
16½	17	2.7	7	6.3	9	7.6			1	.3	10	1.8
17	3	.4	2	1.4	1	.8					1	.2
Total	749		144		131		158		316		605	

[2] Van Denburg, J. K., *The Elimination of Pupils in Public Secondary Schools*, Teachers College, Columbia University, Contributions to Education, No. 47, p. 113, New York, 1911.

those who do not enter high school, the median age ranges from 14.8 to 15.3 years. It is interesting to note that the age increases at about the same interval for each group, beginning with high school graduates. It is a striking fact that Q_1 of the pupils not entering high school is beyond the Q_3 of the high school graduates.

The total number of pupils of the various ages and the percentage of pupils in each group who equal or exceed each of the ages are given in Table XXIII. The same facts for the total number com-

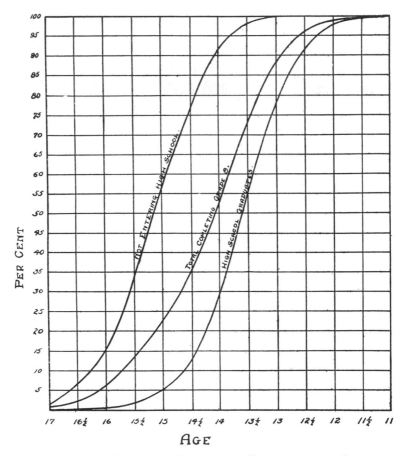

FIGURE 5. CUMULATIVE PERCENTAGE DISTRIBUTION ON BASIS
OF AGE OF TOTAL GROUP COMPLETING GRADE 8, HIGH
SCHOOL GRADUATES, AND GROUP NOT ENTERING
HIGH SCHOOL

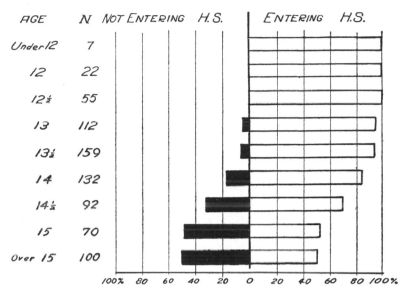

FIGURE 6. PERCENTAGE OF EACH AGE GROUP ENTERING AND
NOT ENTERING HIGH SCHOOL

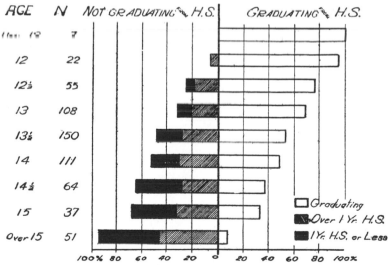

FIGURE 7. PERCENTAGE OF EACH AGE GROUP ENTERING HIGH
SCHOOL WHO DROP OUT OF HIGH SCHOOL, AND PERCENTAGE
WHO GRADUATE

pleting grade 8, the group graduating from high school, and the group not entering high school, are given graphically in Figure 5. The percentage distribution in Figure 6 gives the chances in 100 of a pupil of the various ages when completing grade 8 of not entering high school and of entering high school. For those who enter high school, the percentage distribution in Figure 7 shows the chances in 100 of a pupil of the various ages of dropping out by the end of the first year, of dropping out after one year but before graduating, and of graduating from high school. For example, if a pupil is 12½ years of age at end of grade 8, his chances of entering high school are 100, while they are only half as great if he is 15 years of age at the end of grade 8; furthermore, if he does enter high school at the latter age his chances of dropping out by the end of the first year are six times as great as at the former age, while his chances of graduating are less than half as good.

GRADE-PROGRESS AS A FACTOR IN PERSISTENCE

To what extent is a pupil's rate of progress through the grades a factor that is related to persistence in high school? Figure 8 shows

TABLE XXIV

Distribution of High School Pupils Showing Relation of Grade-Progress to Persistence in High School

Number and Percentage of Pupils of Each Group Equaling or Falling Below Each Condition of Grade-Progress

Grade-Progress	Completing Grade Eight		Not entering High School		High School Entrants							
					One Year		Over One Year		Graduates		Total	
	N	Per cent	N	Per cent	N	Per cent	N	Per cent	N	Per cent	N	Per cent
4	6	100.0							6	100.0	6	100.0
3	26	99.0	2	100.0	4	100.0	5	100.0	15	98.1	24	99.0
2	143	95.5	9	98.6	18	96.9	26	96.8	90	93.4	134	95.1
1	212	76.5	33	92.4	46	83.2	48	80.4	85	64.9	179	72.6
0	219	48.2	44	69.4	35	48.1	51	50.0	89	38.0	175	43.1
—1	91	19.0	36	38.9	17	21.4	16	17.7	22	9.8	55	14.3
—2	39	6.9	14	13.9	7	8.4	11	7.6	7	2.8	25	5.3
—3	11	1.7	4	4.2	4	3.0	1	.6	2	.6	7	1.2
—4	1	.3	1	1.4								
—5	0	.1	0	.7								
—6	1	.1	1	.7								
Total	749		144		131		158		316		605	

the overlapping of the four groups for each of the years, in order. It will be seen that the overlapping on the curve of Group A, high school graduates, is as follows: Group B, over one year in high school but not graduating, 23 per cent, 38 per cent, 31 per cent, and 34 per cent, respectively; Group C, one year or less in high school, 12 per cent, 35 per cent, 35 per cent, and 30 per cent, respectively; and Group D, not entering high school at all, 19 per cent, 18 per cent, 14 per cent, and 26 per cent, respectively. While the overlap-

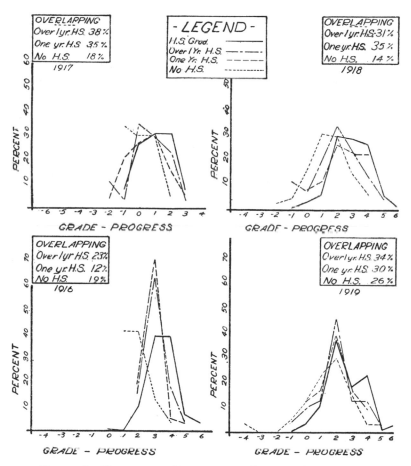

FIGURE 8. PERCENTAGE DISTRIBUTION SHOWING OVERLAPPING OF THE FOUR HIGH SCHOOL GROUPS ON BASIS OF GRADE-PROGRESS

ping is considerable for the first two groups, the small overlapping of the group not going to high school on the group graduating from high school is worthy of note.   Table XXIV shows the cumulative percentage distribution of pupils in various groups on basis of grade-progress for the four years together.   The ogive curves in Figure 9 show how the high school graduates, the group not entering high school, and the entire group completing grade 8, compare in this respect.

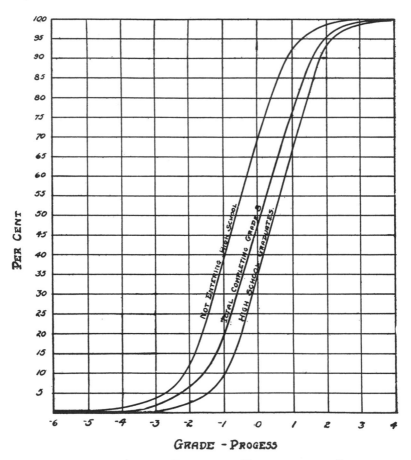

FIGURE 9. CUMULATIVE PERCENTAGE DISTRIBUTION ON BASIS OF
GRADE-PROGRESS OF TOTAL GROUP COMPLETING GRADE 8,
HIGH SCHOOL GRADUATES, AND GROUP NOT ENTERING
HIGH SCHOOL

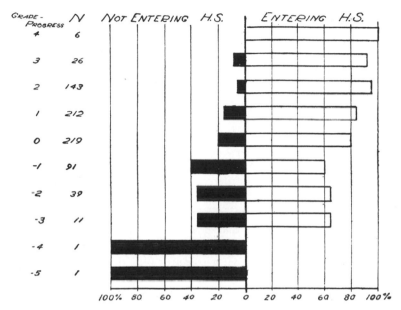

FIGURE 10. PERCENTAGE OF EACH GRADE-PROGRESS GROUP
ENTERING AND NOT ENTERING HIGH SCHOOL

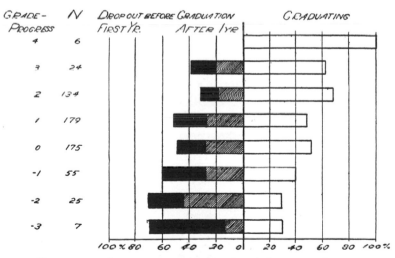

FIGURE 11. PERCENTAGE OF EACH GRADE-PROGRESS GROUP
ENTERING HIGH SCHOOL WHO DROP OUT OF HIGH SCHOOL,
AND PERCENTAGE WHO GRADUATE

The percentage distribution in Figure 10 shows the chances in 100 of a pupil's entering or not entering high school, for pupils ranging from four semesters accelerated to six semesters retarded. In the same way, the percentage distribution of high school entrants in Figure 11 shows the chances in 100 of each of the grade-progress groups of dropping out of high school before the end of the first year, of dropping out of high school after one year but before graduating, and of graduating from high school. These figures show graphically the fact that a pupil's chances of entering high school decrease from 100 when four semesters accelerated to 0 when four semesters retarded; and if he enters high school, his chances of dropping out the first year increase from 0 when four semesters accelerated to 57 when three semesters retarded, whereas the chances of graduating decrease from 100 when four semesters accelerated to 28 when two semesters retarded. Or, in other words, a pupil is six times as likely not to enter high school if he is a year retarded as he is if he is a year accelerated, and if he enters high school he is twice as likely to drop out the first year in the former case as in the latter. Of course, we need not conclude necessarily that the speed with which a pupil progresses through the grades is inherently of such great importance. It is quite likely that there are common causes operating alike to retard a pupil in the grades and to cause him either not to enter high school at all or to drop out before graduating. As to whether these factors are intelligence, traits of character such as persistence or energy, or what not, we venture no opinion, as, obviously, our data throw little light upon that. But, whatever the actual causal factors are, grade-progress and persistence do seem to vary together.

GRADE SCHOOL ACHIEVEMENT AS A FACTOR IN RELATION TO PERSISTENCE

In what respects and to what extent does the grade school achievement of pupils who graduate from high school differ from that of those who do not enter high school, from that of those who remain in high school one year or less, and from that of those who remain in high school longer than one year but never graduate? Table XXV gives the means of these four groups, and the differences between the means of the graduating group and each of the other groups, together with the P.E. of the differences between the means,

TABLE XXV

MEANS IN GRADE SCHOOL ACHIEVEMENT FOR THE FOUR GROUPS,
WITH P.E. OF DIFFERENCES BETWEEN THE GRADUATING
GROUP AND EACH OF THE OTHER GROUPS

Subject	Year	Means of Groups				P.E. of Diff. Between Means		
		A	B	C	D	A–B	A–C	A–D
Reading.........	1916	92	90	88	88	.6	.6	.4
	1917	91	89	90	87	.6	.5	.6
	1918	90	89	87	88	.6	.9	.5
	1919	90	89	87	84	.6	.7	.5
Spelling.........	1916	93	90	89	89	.7	.7	.7
	1917	92	90	90	88	.7	.5	.6
	1918	91	91	87	90	.6	.9	.6
	1919	90	90	88	88	.6	1.0	.7
Arithmetic.......	1916	88	84	84	86	.7	.9	1.0
	1917	87	84	85	85	.7	.6	.6
	1918	86	85	83	83	.5	.8	.7
	1919	85	83	83	82	.7	.7	.8
Geography.......	1916	89	85	86	86	.7	.7	.7
	1917	88	86	86	85	.7	.6	.6
	1918	88	85	84	83	.6	.8	.6
	1919	86	84	83	82	.7	.7	.8
English..........	1916	90	87	85	84	.6	.6	.6
	1917	89	86	85	83	.6	.5	.5
	1918	88	86	84	84	.5	.7	.4
	1919	87	85	85	83	.5	.7	.5
Fine Arts........	1916	88	88	86	86	.5	.5	.6
	1917	88	87	86	85	.5	.5	.5
	1918	86	87	86	86	.4	.5	.3
	1919	87	86	88	85	.4	.6	.5
History..........	1916	90	86	87	86	.7	.6	.8
	1917	88	85	85	85	.7	.6	.8
	1918	88	86	84	83	.6	.8	.7
	1919	87	85	82	83	.8	.8	.7
Special Subjects ..	1916	90	89	89	88	.5	.5	.6
	1917	90	90	89	88	.4	.4	.4
	1918	89	90	89	89	.4	.5	.4
	1919	89	90	90	89	.3	.4	.4
Deportment......	1916	92	91	90	89	.7	.6	.8
	1917	92	90	90	89	.6	.5	.6
	1918	91	91	89	90	.4	.7	.6
	1919	90	91	89	89	.5	.7	.7
Effort..........	1916	93	91	91	91	.5	.5	.5
	1917	93	91	91	90	.5	.4	.4
	1918	92	91	90	90	.4	.6	.5
	1919	92	91	90	90	.5	.6	.6

for the years 1916, 1917, 1918, and 1919. According to the usual statistical practice, a difference between means which is three times the magnitude of its P.E. is considered significant, or reliable. Applying this standard of reliability, we find that the following subjects show significant differences:

Means Compared	Subjects Showing Significant Differences	
	In Every Case	Three Years Out of Four
Group A and Group D	Reading, Geography, English, History, Effort	Spelling, Arithmetic, Fine Arts
Group A and Group C	Geography, English, History, Effort	Spelling, Arithmetic, Reading
Group A and Group B	English	Arithmetic, History, Geography

It is interesting to find that English is the only subject in which there is a significant difference between the means of the graduating group and those of each of the other groups for each of the four years studied, and it will be recalled that this is the subject which had the highest correlation with high school achievement. Most of the other significant factors here also show high correlations with the criteria of high school success (see Table 1).

Another measure of the difference between the groups is the percentage of overlapping. For this purpose the percentage of each group equalling or exceeding the median score of the graduating group is used. Table XXVI gives the medians of the four groups and the overlappings for the years 1916, 1917, 1918, and 1919. As to the significance of these overlappings Thorndike[1] has proposed this standard: "It will be remembered that for practical purposes of school education any percentage between forty and sixty represents a very small difference with very great 'overlapping.'"

[1] Thorndike, E. L., *Educational Psychology, Briefer Course*, Teachers College, Columbia University, p. 345, New York, 1914.

TABLE XXVI

MEDIANS AND PERCENTAGE OF OVERLAPPINGS OF THE FOUR GROUPS

Subject	Year	Medians of Groups				Overlapping on Median of Group A		
		A	B	C	D	B on A	C on A	D on A
Reading.........	1916	93	91	88	88	46	20	10
	1917	92	90	90	87	40	34	19
	1918	91	90	88	88	46	30	26
	1919	91	89	88	85	35	22	17
Spelling..........	1916	94	92	89	90	34	20	27
	1917	93	91	91	88	38	35	19
	1918	92	92	88	90	50	30	40
	1919	90	91	90	89	58	50	49
Arithmetic.......	1916	89	84	84	88	22	33	50
	1917	87	84	85	84	38	44	33
	1918	87	85	84	83	37	26	26
	1919	85	82	83	82	39	34	33
Geography.......	1916	90	85	86	86	22	27	18
	1917	89	86	86	84	30	31	21
	1918	88	85	84	83	35	26	14
	1919	87	85	84	83	42	26	30
English..........	1916	90	87	85	84	34	13	10
	1917	88	86	85	83	38	31	12
	1918	88	86	83	84	42	19	16
	1919	87	85	84	83	39	30	23
Fine Arts........	1916	88	88	86	86	50	33	27
	1917	88	88	86	86	50	38	24
	1918	86	86	86	86	50	50	50
	1919	86	86	87	85	50	70	43
History..........	1916	90	85	87	85	25	33	23
	1917	89	86	86	85	30	31	29
	1918	89	86	83	83	31	19	22
	1919	88	86	82	84	32	17	20
Special Subjects ..	1916	90	90	90	88	50	50	41
	1917	91	90	89	89	46	29	31
	1918	89	90	89	90	66	50	66
	1919	90	90	90	89	50	50	49
Deportment......	1916	93	92	92	90	44	43	27
	1917	93	91	90	90	43	36	29
	1918	91	92	90	91	63	41	50
	1919	91	91	90	91	50	44	50
Effort..........	1916	94	91	92	91	25	33	23
	1917	93	91	91	90	43	35	26
	1918	92	92	91	91	50	45	46
	1919	92	91	90	91	48	35	47

Applying this standard, we find that the following subjects show significant differences:

Overlapping of Groups	Significant Differences as Shown by Overlapping	
	In Every Case	Three Years Out of Four
Group D on Group A	Reading, Geography, English, History	Arithmetic
Group C on Group A	Reading, Geography, English, History	Spelling, Arithmetic, Fine Arts, Effort
Group B on Group A	Arithmetic, History	Geography, English

As both the differences between means and the overlappings agree upon these same factors, we are justified in thinking them significant. Figure 12 shows graphically the overlappings of the four groups in each of these eight factors for the year, 1917.

ATTENDANCE IN THE GRADE SCHOOL AS A FACTOR IN
RELATION TO PERSISTENCE IN HIGH SCHOOL

To what extent does the attendance record in the grade school of those pupils who subsequently graduate from high school differ from that of those who do not enter high school at all, from that of those who remain in high school for one year or less, and from that of those who remain in high school longer than one year but do not graduate? As to the effect of attendance upon a pupil's school achievement, considerable difference of opinion exists. For example, Strayer and Thorndike[1] say: "The effect of absence is small until very large amounts of absence have been reached." On the other hand, Reavis[2] concludes from his study of two hundred country schools in Maryland, "A pupil's progress in a rural school seems to be a function of his attendance. His standing in the class with which he recites has a definite and fixed relation to the number of days he is present. . . . Thus attendance in one year, by affecting a pupil's class standing, also affects his future attendance."

[1] Strayer, G. D., and Thorndike, E. L., *Educational Administration*, p. 42, The Macmillan Company, New York, 1914.
[2] Reavis, *op. cit.*, p. 17.

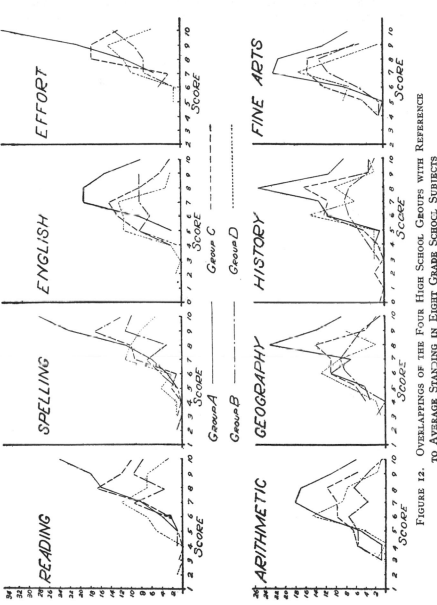

FIGURE 12. OVERLAPPINGS OF THE FOUR HIGH SCHOOL GROUPS WITH REFERENCE
TO AVERAGE STANDING IN EIGHT GRADE SCHOOL SUBJECTS

The average daily attendance of the four groups under consideration in this study, grades two to eight inclusive, are given below for the years 1916, 1917, 1918, and 1919.

Year	Average Attendance				P.E. of Difference Between Means		
	A	B	C	D	B−A	C−A	D−A
1916	174	175	179	179	1.3	1.0	1.2
1917	176	178	179	179	1.2	.9	1.0
1918	175	180	179	178	1.2	1.5	1.1
1919	170	174	172	174	1.1	1.4	1.1

It is interesting to note that in every case the average daily attendance of the high school graduates (Group A) is exceeded by that of the other groups, the difference being from one to five days. Although this difference is small, the ratio of the difference to its P.E. indicates that the difference between the graduate group and the group not entering high school is significant in three of the four years, and very nearly so the other year. Any explanation of this would be mere conjecture, but possible guesses are that pupils who are absent a very great deal never even finish the grade school, and that wise parents sometimes keep their children at home a day or so now and then for perfectly justifiable reasons. But whatever the explanation of the situation found here, the fact is clear *of the pupils completing grade 8*, the attendance record in the grade school is but a slight factor in relation to length of stay in high school.

IS THE QUALITY OF HIGH SCHOOL PUPILS DETERIORATING?

Thorndike[1] estimates that in 1918 one in three children reaching their teens enter high school, while a corresponding figure for 1890 would not be over one in ten. His conclusions are significant, "We lack measures of the inborn capacities of the one in ten or eleven of a generation ago and have only very scanty measures of the capacities of the one in three of to-day. We have, however, excellent reasons for believing that the one in ten had greater capacities for

[1] Thorndike, E. L., "Quality of Pupils Entering High School," *School Review*, Vol. XXX, No. 5, p. 357, May, 1920.

algebra and for intellectual tasks generally than the one in three of to-day."

Let us now compare the average grade school achievements shown in Table XXV of the high school graduates for the years 1916, 1917, 1918, 1919, in certain representative subjects: Reading, 92, 91, 90, 90; spelling, 93, 92, 91, 90; arithmetic, 89, 87, 86, 85; geography, 89, 88, 88, 86; English, 90, 89, 88, 87. Here we note that the average grade school mark in these subjects has shown a consistent decrease from year to year. In general, the same is true for the other subjects as well. It may be instructive to compare the corresponding averages for these years of the pupils not entering high school, which are, respectively: Reading, 88, 87, 88, 84; spelling, 89, 88, 90, 88; arithmetic, 86, 85, 83, 82; geography, 86, 85, 83, 82; English, 84, 83, 84, 83. It will be noted that the average of these pupils not entering high school has also decreased somewhat during this period, which indicates that the quality of pupils completing grade 8 has been declining, which explains the decrease in the quality of the high school graduates, as an increasingly large proportion of pupils completing grade 8 enter high school and finally graduate. It seems likely, therefore, that the high school still continues to select the pupils who make the superior records in the grade school, and, perhaps, there is *relatively* as much difference between high school pupils and other pupils as ever, although the *absolute* quality of the former has probably declined.

Owing to the close relationship repeatedly shown by this and other studies between youth and academic success, additional evidence bearing upon this point is afforded by Figure 4, which shows that the median age at the time of completing grade 8 of pupils who later graduate from high school has been increasing year by year, while the median age of the other groups has been steadily declining.

CAN WE PREDICT A PUPIL'S LENGTH OF STAY IN HIGH SCHOOL?

.It is of interest to discover in what respects and to what extent the grade school record of the pupils who graduate from high school differs from that of those who do not enter high school at all, from that of those who remain in high school one year or less, and that of those who remain longer than one year in high school but do not graduate. It is of even greater interest, however, to know to what extent a pupil's probable length of stay in high school can be predicted from his grade school record.

To ascertain this the correlation was obtained between each of the factors that had previously been found significant in predicting academic achievement in high school and the number of semesters spent in the high school. In these correlations a pupil not entering high school is regarded as having spent 0 semesters in high school; and a pupil is regarded as having spent 8 semesters in high school, if he has been in high school four full years or more, or if he has graduated from high school, although he may have completed the course in three years. In other words, 8 semesters represent the full four years' course, and it is not thought wise to regard a longer stay as more desirable than the normal length. Our problem is, therefore, to find to what extent we can predict the number of semesters a pupil will remain in high school, up to and including 8 semesters, the normal time for graduation. Table XXVII gives the correlation with number of semesters in high school for the year 1917 of the twelve factors already found of most significance for predicting academic achievement in the high school.

TABLE XXVII

CORRELATION OF TWELVE MOST SIGNIFICANT FACTORS WITH
LENGTH OF STAY IN HIGH SCHOOL

Grade School Factor	Correlation with Semesters in High School
Age at End of Gr. 8*...............	.57
Grade-Progress.....................	.32
Arithmetic, Gr. 7–8................	.19
English, Gr. 4–6...................	.29
English, Gr. 7–8...................	.37
History, Gr. 5–6..................	.23
History, Gr. 7–8..................	.21
Spec. Subjects, Gr. 4–6	.18
Spec. Subjects, Gr. 7–8	.10
Effort, Gr. 7–8....................	.27
Days Present, Gr. 2–3.............	.04
Days Present, Gr. 4–6.............	—.21

* Age here is regarded as *youth;* that is, the oldest pupil is in the zero class and the youngest pupil is in the highest class.

Our next problem is to discover what combination of these factors will yield the highest measure of prediction of persistence in high school. Again applying the method of multiple correlations we determine what this optimum combination of factors is, and at what weight each factor enters into the composite. The results are given in Table XXVIII. Age at completing grade 8 is by far the most significant factor, the correlations being .61, .57, .50, and .51, for the years, 1916, 1917, 1918, and 1919, respectively, and it enters into the composite with a weight of 10. It will be seen that two of these factors, age at completing grade 8, and days present, grades 4–6, are entirely objective in character, while the other two represent teachers' marks for the last two years of grade school. Of these subjective factors, one, English, is a measure of language ability, and the other, effort, has to do with the pupil's attitude toward his work and the school organization in general. One might expect that grade-progress, with a correlation of .32 with the criterion, would enter into the composite. The reason why it does not do so is because of the high interrelationship between age and grade-progress. While grade-progress correlates .32 with persistence in high school, it correlates .45 with age, the most important factor in the composite. By partial correlations it is found that age, when freed from any connection with grade-progress, still correlates .50 with the composite, whereas grade-progress, when freed from its connection with age, drops from .32 to .09. This illustrates the point that a factor to be added to the composite must measure some ability not measured by factors already in the composite.

TABLE XXVIII

The Weights of the Four Grade School Factors Entering into the Composite for Predicting Persistence in High School

Correlation of Composite with Persistence = .63 $N = 200$

Factor	True β	S.D.	$\dfrac{\text{True } \beta}{\text{S.D.}}$	Approximate Weight
Age at End Gr. 8.....	1.0000	2.155	.4640	10
English, Gr. 7–8......	.1898	1.970	.0963	2
Effort, Gr. 7–8........	.2988	1.553	.1924	4
Days Present, Gr. 4–6.	−.3862	.977	−.3952	−8

These four grade school factors, when combined at the weights indicated, correlate with the number of semesters in high school to the extent of .63 for the year 1917. When this formula was applied to the other years the following results were obtained:

Year	N	r
1916	141	.63
1917	200	.63
1918	214	.52
1919	194	.54

Although correlations of this magnitude are not high enough to be of much value in predicting the chances of any particular individual's probable length of stay in high school, they do indicate that the relationship between the grade school record and persistence in high school are both fairly high and relatively consistent from year to year.

SUMMARY AND CONCLUSIONS

What, then, can we say of the relation between a pupil's record in the grade school and his persistence in high school? The following conclusions seem warranted by the facts presented in this chapter:

1. The grade school record of those pupils who graduate from high school differs from that of those who do not enter high school, from that of those who remain in high school one year or less, and from that of those who continue in high school longer than one year but who do not graduate, in the following respects: They are younger, have progressed through the grades more rapidly, and have a better grade-school record in spelling, reading, arithmetic, geography, history, English, fine arts, and effort.

2. The most significant single factor in relation to persistence in high school is the age at completing grade 8, which correlates with semesters spent in high school for the years 1916, 1917, 1918, and 1919, to the extent of .61, .57, .50, and .51, respectively.

3. A composite score made up of age at completing grade 8, average days present, grades 4–6, average English mark, grades 7–8, and average mark in effort, grades 7–8, correlates with number of semesters spent in high school for the years 1916, 1917, 1918, and 1919, to the extent of .63, .63, .52, .54, respectively.

CHAPTER V

GENERAL SUMMARY AND CONCLUSIONS

1. This is a study of the relation between high school achievement and the various factors that appear on the individual record cards of pupils at the time of completing grade 8. All pupils are included who completed grade 8 for four successive years in one city and who have been in the school system from the beginning of the third grade, seven hundred forty-nine pupils all told.

2. Answers to two major questions have been sought: First, what is the relation between a pupil's grade school record and his subsequent academic record in high school? Second, what is the relation between a pupil's grade school record and his length of stay in high school?

3. The correlations have been found between each of the factors of the grade school record and average standing in the first year of high school, and standing in the individual subjects, English, Latin, and mathematics. Afterward the combinations of these factors that yield the highest correlation with the three criteria of first year high school success have been determined. In the same way the combination of factors that would best predict average standing of pupils who remain two or more years in high school, and the combination that would best predict average English standing of pupils who remain two or more years in high school, have been obtained. These results may be summarized as follows:

a. The factors of the grade school record vary widely in their relation to high school success. The correlations with average standing in the first year of high school range from −.36 to .56; with English the range is from −.38 to .54; with Latin the range is from −.25 to .54; and with mathematics the range is from −.26 to .42. The median correlations are, respectively, .33, .39, .24, and .15.

b. The factors which enter into the various composites, together with their respective class-interval weights, are given in Table XXIX.

TABLE XXIX

FACTORS OF THE GRADE SCHOOL RECORD WHICH ENTER INTO THE
COMPOSITE SCORES FOR PREDICTING HIGH SCHOOL ACHIEVEMENT,
WITH THEIR CLASS-INTERVAL WEIGHTS

Factor	Weights of Factors in Various Composites					
	First Year High School Success				Average Success (2–4 Years)	
	General Average	English	Latin	Mathematics	Total	English
Age at end Gr. 8....	−3	−6	−5		−3	
Grade-Progress......			7	5	7	
English, Gr. 4–6.....	6	10		7	9	10
English, Gr. 7–8.....		10	10		7	6
Arithmetic, Gr. 7–8..	4		4	9	9	
Spec. Subjects, Gr. 7–8		6		−7		7
History, Gr. 5–6.....			10			
History, Gr. 7–8.....						7
Effort, Gr. 7–8......	6				5	
Days Present, Gr. 2–3			−5	5		
Days Present, Gr. 4–6	−4		−9			

TABLE XXX

SUMMARY OF CORRELATIONS OF GRADE SCHOOL COMPOSITE SCORES
WITH HIGH SCHOOL ACHIEVEMENT

Grade School Composite	First Year High School Achievement					Average Achievement (Two or More Years)			
	New Rochelle, New York				Des Moines, Iowa				
	1916	1917	1918	1919	1922	1916	1917	1918	1919
General Average.	.68	.67	.56	.65	.69	.60	.64	.57	.66
English.........	.60	.67	.67	.60	.61	.62	.67	.52	.60
Latin..........	.58	.73	.57	.64	.61	...	...	...	...
Mathematics....	.42	.51	.43	.51	.51	...	...	...	...

c. The multiple equations were obtained from the data of the year 1917. These equations were afterwards applied to the similar data for the year preceding, and the two years following that date in the same situation, and then to the data of a wholly different situation five years later. The resulting correlations appear in Table XXX.

4. The study also attempts to discover in what respects and to what extent the grade school records of pupils who graduate from high school differ from those of pupils who remain in high school longer than one year but do not graduate, from those of pupils who remain one year or less in high school, and from those of pupils who complete grade 8 but do not enter high school at all. The study also seeks to find to what extent a pupil's length of stay in high school can be predicted from his grade school record. The results may be summarized as follows:

a. The pupils who graduate from high school differ from the other groups in the following respects: They are younger; they have progressed through the grades more rapidly; and they have a better grade-school record in spelling, reading, arithmetic, English, geography, history, fine arts, and effort.

b. The most significant single factor in relation to persistence in high school is the pupil's age at completing grade 8, which correlates with semesters spent in high school of the groups completing grade 8 in the years 1916, 1917, 1918, and 1919 to the extent of .61, .57, .50, and .51, respectively.

c. A composite score made up of age at completing grade 8, average days present, grades 4–6, average English mark, grades 7–8, and average mark in effort, grades 7–8, with weights of 10, 2, 4, and −8, respectively, correlates with semesters spent in high school as follows: 1916 group, .63; 1917 group, .63; 1918 group, .52; 1919 group, .54.

5. The findings of this study warrant the following conclusions:

a. The correlations between the grade school record and high school achievement are sufficiently high to be significant, being in most cases higher than the corresponding correlations between standard test scores and high school achievement.

b. The correlations between the grade school record and high school achievement are sufficiently stable to be reliable, having established their claim to stability by showing remarkable consistency for four years in one city and for one year in another city.

c. The correlations between the grade school record and persistence in high school are fairly high and relatively consistent from year to year.

d. The pupil's individual grade school record card should provide a definite place for entering the average rating on the significant factors by grade-groups, and for the total composite rating for each of the high school subjects for which a prediction may be sought. These composite ratings should become an integral part of the pupil's credentials when he is promoted to high school, and should be made available for vocational and educational counsellors, grade school principals, high school principals, and all administrative officials whose duty it may be to provide for the subsequent education of these pupils.

e. The best basis for predicting high school achievement would seem to be a combination of the following: (1) Intelligence test ratings, which would afford a measure of the pupil's native endowment; (2) ratings on standard achievement tests, which would afford objective evidence as to the pupil's prerequisite academic preparation, and which would make possible ready comparisons between different teachers and different schools; (3) and teachers' ratings in the grade school, which afford a measure of the pupil's attitudes and habits of character, such as industry, persistence and conscientiousness, already acquired, factors which have been reflected in the grade school record, and which will always be very important factors in determining an individual's success in school and out of school.